KABBALAH AND PSYCHOANALYSIS

KABBALAH AND PSYCHOANALYSIS

Michael Eigen

KARNAC

First published in 2012 by
Karnac Books Ltd
118 Finchley Road, London NW3 5HT

Copyright © 2012 to Michael Eigen.

The right of Michael Eigen to be identified as the author of this work has been asserted in accordance with §§ 77 and 78 of the Copyright Design and Patents Act 1988.

All rights reserved. No part of this publication may be reproduced, stored in a retrieval system, or transmitted, in any form or by any means, electronic, mechanical, photocopying, recording, or otherwise, without the prior written permission of the publisher.

British Library Cataloguing in Publication Data

A C.I.P. for this book is available from the British Library

ISBN 978 1 78049 080 9

Edited, designed and produced by The Studio Publishing Services Ltd
www.publishingservicesuk.co.uk
e-mail: studio@publishingservicesuk.co.uk

Printed in Great Britain

www.karnacbooks.com

CONTENTS

ABOUT THE AUTHOR	vii
PREFACE AND INTRODUCTION	ix
CHAPTER ONE	1
CHAPTER TWO	39
Appendix 1: *Ein Sof* and the *Sephirot* (Tree of Life)	79
Appendix 2: Four worlds	93
Appendix 3: Circle and rays	97
Appendix 4: O-grams	101
Appendix 5: Bion's Grid	107
Appendix 6: Bion quotes	115
Appendix 7: Rabbi Nachman's paths	125
Appendix 8: Selected readings	129
REFERENCES	133
INDEX	137

I use the Kabbalah as a framework for psychoanalysis.

(W. R. Bion)

To tear even three letters from a page of Torah, put them in your mouth and taste, your tongue will burn like the child Moses with a holy fire that never goes out. The fire that never goes out meets the wound that never heals.

(Michael Eigen)

Weeping is lodged in one side of my heart, and joy is lodged in the other.

(*The Zohar*)

I go out to seek You and find You coming towards me.

(Yehudah Halevi)

Nothing is more whole than a broken heart.

(Rabbi Nachman)

There is something about going into the depths, and even further, beyond what we think the depths can be.

(Merle Molofsky)

My cup runneth over.

(Psalm 23)

Open heart, mind breathes.

ABOUT THE AUTHOR

Michael Eigen worked with disturbed, especially psychotic, children in his twenties, then with adults in his thirties onwards. He directed an institute program for working with creative individuals at the Center for Psychoanalytic Training and was the first Director of Educational Training at the Institute for Expressive Analysis. He was on the Board of Directors at the National Psychological Association for Psychoanalysis for eight years, first as Program Chair, then editor of *The Psychoanalytic Review*. He taught at many institutes and colleges and gave talks and seminars internationally. For the past twenty years he has taught and supervised mainly at the National Psychological Association for Psychoanalysis and the New York University Postdoctoral Program in Psychotherapy and Psychoanalysis. He has given private seminars on Winnicott, Bion, Lacan and his own work, over thirty-five years and still ongoing. *Kabbalah and Psychoanalysis* is his twenty-first book. It is based on recent seminars given for the New York University Contemplative Studies Project.

To

Shirah Kober Zeller and Jerry Zeller

Vision and support

ABOUT THE AUTHOR

Michael Eigen worked with disturbed, especially psychotic, children in his twenties, then with adults in his thirties onwards. He directed an institute program for working with creative individuals at the Center for Psychoanalytic Training and was the first Director of Educational Training at the Institute for Expressive Analysis. He was on the Board of Directors at the National Psychological Association for Psychoanalysis for eight years, first as Program Chair, then editor of *The Psychoanalytic Review*. He taught at many institutes and colleges and gave talks and seminars internationally. For the past twenty years he has taught and supervised mainly at the National Psychological Association for Psychoanalysis and the New York University Postdoctoral Program in Psychotherapy and Psychoanalysis. He has given private seminars on Winnicott, Bion, Lacan and his own work, over thirty-five years and still ongoing. *Kabbalah and Psychoanalysis* is his twenty-first book. It is based on recent seminars given for the New York University Contemplative Studies Project.

To
Shirah Kober Zeller and Jerry Zeller
Vision and support

Preface and Introduction

This book grew out of two seminars on Kabbalah and psychoanalysis given for the New York University Postdoctoral Contemplative Studies Project (10 October 2010 and 3 April 2011) at the suggestion of Dr James Ogilvie. Daniel Wentworth transcribed the tapes of these seminars. I have added some new material without disturbing the flow of the seminar as it happened. The Appendices stand as a little book in itself. I think of how enthralled I was with the appendix to Marion Milner's *On Not Being Able to Paint*, which opens dimensions only hinted at in the text. That remains as a background model for the importance of what is added on.

Part of the impetus for this work, although I did not suspect it then, was a spontaneous interchange I had with Wilfred R. Bion in 1978, the year before he died. We were speaking, and out of the blue he asked, "Do you know the Kabbalah, the Zohar?" As far as I was aware, there was no preparation for this remark. He just said it. I was a bit taken aback and said, "Well, I know it, but don't really *know* it." I read bits of Kabbalah since my early twenties and, without conscious awareness, it was part of my lived background from early childhood. I was in my early forties when I met Bion. He quickly said, "I don't either, really know it," modestly reassuring me. It was established that neither of us were scholars, experts, "knowers", but had awareness, acquaintance. There was a pause. Then he looked at me and said, "I use the Kabbalah as a framework for psychoanalysis."

I said nothing for a while, letting the remark sink in. I remembered a seminar with Joseph Campbell, who used the Kundalini chakras as a framework for Freud and Jung and varied reaches of spiritual life, so, although I was surprised, I was not totally surprised. Yet, hearing Bion say this set off ripples. I wondered for years why he said that to me. As far as I have been able to learn so far, I did not hear of him saying that to anyone else. Why me?

A few years later, reading one of his Brazilian seminars, I found a passage in which he spoke about a Jewish patient who devalued his racial background. He was supervising a case and spoke about the patient's attitude as cutting him off from something basic, a font of potential richness. This cutting off stifled a basic flow of his being. I wondered if Bion's remark about Kabbalah was meant to stimulate, invite, nourish my Jewish soul? Did it imply something about my own need to become at-one with a profound source of possibility in my being, one I partly disowned, brushed past, neglected? Our conversations accomplished a lot in a short time (Eigen & Govrin, 2007) and some of what happened took years to bear fruit. This book is one of the outcomes, thirty-four years later.

I am not a Kabbalah scholar, but aspects of its teachings have become part of me, as has psychoanalytic work. The two have many points of convergence. The main psychoanalytic writer I use in this work is Bion, partly because of his striking statement that he uses Kabbalah as a framework for psychoanalysis, but largely because it is hard to miss connections between the two. Both are preoccupied with catastrophe and faith. Bion calls faith the psychoanalytic attitude. Both are preoccupied with infinity and intensity of experience. Both are preoccupied with shatter and the possibility of bearing and growing the kind of psyche that can work with the dimensions sensitivity opens. Both are preoccupied with ontological implications of the Unknown and the importance of emotional life. Bion, too, writes penetratingly about an ongoing crises of faith, basic to Kabbalah concerns.

As in all of my work, D. W. Winnicott plays an important background role. His writings on vital sparks connect with Kabbalah's buried divine sparks scattered everywhere. His incommunicado core connects with Kabbalah's *Ein Sof*, the infinite beyond bounds and conception. For Winnicott, too, faith is important, what I call a paradoxical faith (Eigen, 1998) because it spans and opens diverse dimensions without reductively taking sides. Winnicott also writes of the importance of creative illusion, which adds to richness of living, even helps one feel alive. He locates illusion in transitional experiencing, which takes different forms as one grows. It might be that what we call self is, partly, a transitional state, which, like dolls, games, hobbies of childhood, lose meaning as one grows. We outgrow self-identities once treasured as new dimensions of experience open and take us forward. Yet, paradoxically, old self-states might deepen when we touch them with who we are now.

The present work is my own exploration supported by many sources. The writing on Rabbi Nachman in Chapter Two draws heavily from Arthur Green's (1992) *Tormented Master: The Life and Spiritual Quest of Rabbi Nahman of Bratslav*. It is also enriched by Rodger Kamenetz's (2010) *Burnt Books: Rabbi Nachman of Bratslav and Franz Kafka*. The different spellings of Nachman/Nahman are discussed in Appendix 7: "Rabbi Nachman's paths". My thanks to Dr Sue Saperstein for urging me to read the above works by Green and Kamenetz.

I list some suggested readings in Appendix 8, in addition to the References, but no short list can cover the ground. Some of my most important learnings were from direct exposure to teachers and life itself. The Kabbalah is not a unified work, but a loose term that covers an archipelago of possibilities, texts from many times and places and many personalities one can only imagine. My own life has been touched by a diversity of spiritual–mystical traditions besides Judaism, including Buddhist, Taoist, Hindu, Sufi, and Christian. Similarly, a host of psychoanalytic and non-analytic influences are important to me, including Freud, Jung, Adler, Reich, Searles, Elkin, Kohut, Bion, Winnicott, Milner, Lacan, Perls, and various kinds of body work. I would list a host of *simpatico* contemporaries, but am in dread of leaving someone out. I am not an expert in anything, but I am grateful to many contacts for opening aspects of reality.

For many, a sense of infinity interweaves with everyday life. They are part of each other, one reality. This interweaving has been part of my life ever since I can remember and helped make my life meaningful beyond words. Sometimes, I picture individuals and humankind as a whole as a mansion with many rooms, many of which we may never enter. Perhaps this is one source of dreams of houses or apartments that show us more rooms than we imagined. We often need support, permission to occupy some of these unknown spaces, to enter creative relationship with the more we did not know we were.

Texts can be like living organisms, at times, more real than life. I hope this book takes you to places you value, opens possibilities, and supports the unfolding of your own sensibility.

CHAPTER ONE

[Testing microphone, chanting]: Shema. Shhhmaaaa. Shhhh . . .

The heart of the Kabbalah, the very heart of Kabbalah is the line: "*V'ahav'ta eit Adonai Elohekha b'khol l'vav'kha uv'khol naf'sh'kha uv'khol m'odekha*". Everyone who knows this line please say it with me. (Group: *V'ahav'ta eit Adonai Elohekha b'khol l'vav'kha uv'khol naf'sh'kha uv'khol m'odekha.*) (*Deuteronomy* 6:5.)

When I was a child, we were taught that this meant, "You will love the Lord your God with all your heart, with all your soul, with all your might." It was presented as a commandment, although, even as a child, I felt there was more to it. More resonance, another vibration I could not quite link up with: more than a commandment, other than a commandment. It was a clue about who I was and what was in me.

When I was a little older, I took it as an invitation: you are *invited* to love God with all your heart and soul and might. A sort of invitation to God's playground, God's holy ground. You are invited to come and play with God with all your heart and soul and might. Then, when I was still older, I started thinking, *V'ahav'ta*—and you will love. And you *will* love, you will *love*. When I am in despair and wretched and totally unloving and hateful and miserable and have no guidance or hope, something sometimes comes up in me and says, "I love you." And it is the hope that I *will* love. You *will* love, you will love God with all your heart and soul and might.

When I became older still, I began to sense this sentence as a statement of fact. It was just the way it was, it is the way we are imprinted. It is something in us, something in our foundation, a blueprint for our very being. It keeps changing, opening. One never stops growing into it. We relate to it differently at different times, and it relates to us differently. It is a statement of fact. I love you. I love God with all my heart and soul and might. So let's say that together: "I love God with all my heart and soul and might." (Group: I love God with all my heart and soul and might. I love God with all my heart and soul and might.) I love you. I love you. I love you with all my heart and soul and might: a commandment, an invitation, a challenge, a fact. The heart of both Kabbalah and Torah. Everything grows out of this love.

The *you* in the words "and you will" is an inclusive you, meaning all of us. *V'ahav'ta eit Adonai* ("and you will love the Lord"). *Adonai*, as many of you know, is a substitute word. *Adonai* means "lord", and it substitutes for the *tetragrammaton, Yud-Hay-Vav-Hay*. Throughout the Torah, *Yud-Hay-Vav-Hay (YHVH)* is the word that is used. But then, superimposed on it is *Adonai*.

You are not supposed to say the tetragrammaton, YHVH. We do not even know how it is said, We do not know the vowel sounds, although early Christian texts tell us you say it, "Yahweh". Sometimes, in wry, humorous moments, I think maybe it was pronounced Oy-vey, or something that led to this all purpose expression. A few days ago, I stopped some very religious looking Jews in the park and asked them about words for God that were singular and plural. In their answer, they used the word Jaweh—avoiding pronunciation of Y and V. With Jaweh, you almost say the name without saying the name. Jaweh: close but not quite. Who knows?

Here is a semi-Kabbalistic story. When I was a child in Passaic, New Jersey, a man from New York would come and visit us once or twice a year seeking a charitable donation for the poor of his Chassidic group. His name was Rabbi Kellner and he always had a nice word for me, a little boy. When I saw him, something different happened from the usual person I would meet in Passaic. His face had a glow and I did not know what the glow was. It did something special inside. When I grew up, I came to know the glow was a sense of the holy. When Rabbi Kellner came, my father stopped whatever he was doing. I do not remember much of what was said, but the feeling never left. (Aner Govrin questioned me about my childhood in Passaic, New Jersey, and you can find out about it in *Conversations With Michael Eigen*, 2007.)

When my father died in 1986 I went to a *shul* (synagogue, temple, house of prayer and study) near my house in Brooklyn to say kaddish. I picked this *shul* because, weeks before, the rabbi from this *shul* was walking down the street with a *lulav* and *esrog* and invited my five-year-old son and I to say a prayer and shake them. (The *lulav* is a bundle of palm, myrtle and willow; the *esrog* a citrus similar to a lemon. You shake them all around you, God all around you, celebrating Sukkot, holiday of huts and fall harvest, remembering the trek through the wilderness, underscoring impermanence and deep dependence on God.) My son and I enjoyed shaking them. It felt so good that when I went to say kaddish, I picked this rabbi's *shul*. Not long before my father died, he told me the kaddish is not what many think, a mourning prayer, a sad prayer—it is a song of praise, it sings God's praises. He meant me to say kaddish in this fashion.

About the same time I started going to my neighbourhood *shul*, a rabbi who spoke at my father's funeral in Passaic put me in contact with Rabbi Kastel in Crown Heights, Brooklyn. I spent some time with Rabbi Kastel and when he heard my story about Rabbi Kellner, he fixed me up with Rabbi Kellner's two sons, then old men living in Crown Heights. So there I was, a man in my fifties, studying with Rabbi Kellner's sons in Brooklyn. There is much to tell you about these weekly visits, but that will have to wait for another day. I was lucky to have the time with them that I did, for, not long after we stopped, they left this earth. If that's not Kabbalistic, I don't know . . . The rabbi whose *shul* I picked in my neighbourhood also had roots in Crown Heights—again, stories for another day.

Time does strange things. It opens doors you do not expect to be opened. Doors close, doors open.

Here is a little something the Kellners taught me. I asked them, in the *sh'ma*, why are there two names of God, Yahweh and Elohenu (*Sh'ma Yisroel, Adonai Elohenu, Adonai echad*: Hear, O Israel, the Lord is our God, the Lord is one. Adonai, lord, is orally substituted for the written YHVH, the unsayable infinite mystery). They told me one is singular and one is plural. YHVH—adonai, lord—singular. Elohenu plural, gods. In my mind—and they did not correct me—I took it that all the gods, all the gods the Bible alludes to, or that anyone might allude to, all are subsumed by the One, profiles of the One, so to speak. The One and Only remaining beyond thought, image, word. All gods are One God, with the mystery of the One taking precedence. Plural and singular are one. A unity of plurality and the One.

The *one* runs through religions, doesn't it? There is a one in Taoism. In Buddhism, there is one-finger Zen, our original face, and much more. At rock concerts, everyone waves their hand above their head with their index finger pointing upward. At Matisyahu (a Chassidic rocker-rapper) concerts, the same thing happens, all the people in the room waving one finger upward in time with the music. So this one is very special, very popular. All one. When I think on it now, I get a sense that I am honoured to be here. It is an honour to be with you. And it is an honour for us to be here at all. The Dalai Lama talks about the precious human form, and my prayer is that we honour the day and that the day honours us, that we are worthy of life this day and that life gives us inspiration to go forward, to open a little more.

It is one of the themes in Kabbalah, and one of the themes in aspects of psychoanalysis, that we are broken. And, at the same time, there is an odd paradox—a kind of paradoxical monism rather than dualism—that we are whole and broken at the same time. Psalms tell us that the soul is pure and kabbalah adds that there is a soul point in contact with God at all times. We might or might not be aware of this point of contact. A term like "point" is just an image for ineffable sense of contact with the Deepest of All. Yet, the psalms also tell us of times when we feel no contact, bereft of contact, abandoned, abysmal, and long for contact again. I said before that we are touching something more than duality, but, paradoxically, we are deep in dualities. I am and am not in contact with God. We are and are not in contact. Something in me might be pure, I am not pure. I can be a devil. I am mischievous, weird, playful, nasty, selfish, and worse, yet I have to bear witness to something pure, whole, utterly uplifting and amazing: a miracle that a life form such as you and me should be. Crippled and whole, corrupt and pure, and everything between and mixed. I would like to touch the theme of brokenness more.

Kabbalah is vast. Kabbalah is not a unified thing, an official set of books like the Torah. It is an archipelago, fragments over time. That one wrote this, this one wrote that. It accumulates over many years, possibly to this day. Many tracts, books, visions, meditations, records of talks, probably spanning more than 2,000 years, reaching back to imaginative elaborations of what Torah is made of, hidden, deeper meanings. Kabbalah reaches us through broken forms touching a needy core. It is about a deep intimacy we sense and express, lose, re-find, re-create in longing, suffering, and rejoicing.

One thread on brokenness that has become a popular Kabbalah theme is in Lurianic Kabbalah. Rabbi Isaac Luria taught in Safed in the sixteenth century. He did not write much, but a follower, Chaim Vital, wrote and reshaped his talks and teachings. I will share a little portion of his vision, which many of you know. We all have our idiosyncratic ways of telling a story. God felt inspired to create something. It is odd to say this about God, since creativity, we imagine, is intrinsic to his "nature". The God of *Genesis* is, if anything, a creative God. In the beginning, God created or, to change it to something a little more like an ideogram: In the beginning God creating. Or leave out "in" and "the": Beginning God Creating.

Perhaps God felt a need to share creative being, although, again, the word "need" sounds suspect when it comes to certain views of God. In Kabbalah, God is often talked about as having needs, although one realises one is speaking about the unspeakable. To speak of need is to speak of love; to share creativity out of love, or simply out of creativeness as such.

Some Gnostic teachings tell us that creation is a kind of step down for God, a lower form of God's being. There are Kabbalah teachings that echo this, but there are others that give a special weight to this "lower" creation, a place of radical consequence, filled with spiritual possibility, a place where compassion can be realised, as compassion and cruelty vie and intertwine. Life as home to anguish and joy.

A problem God faced: how to go about creating something if you are everything? There is no room for creation if God fills everything. God's problem is how to make room for anything but God. Rabbi Luria (1534–1572) in Safed and Jacob Boehme, a German mystic born two years after Rabbi Luria died, had similar solutions. God contracts to make room for the world. I wonder if this is a kind of mystical underpinning for Martha Graham's emphasis on contraction. I say this somewhat tongue in cheek because contraction has many possibilities, as in contracting with pain and anguish, or, more Taoist, part of the in-out rhythm of breath, or Melanie Klein's unconscious phantasy processes involving introjection–projection. We even speak of expanding–contracting universes. Then there is the wordplay, the double meaning of contract, to pull in, to make a contract with, a covenant.

God pulls back, contracts. I see it as a bow: bowing, making room for the other. Making space, a covenant, a kind of mutual bowing. Now, everything we say about God, we are saying about ourselves. We say God is omniscient, omnipotent, but these are capacities we wish for ourselves. More, we act as if we *are* omniscient and omnipotent in important ways. That is, we act as if we know everything, or more than we do, and that we have power to do whatever we want, or are deluded to think so. Omniscience and omnipotence as powerful fantasies that permeate our behaviour, often with disastrous results, sometimes with astonishing creative results. As analysts, we might say we project omniscience–omnipotence on to God, reflecting our own preoccupation with knowledge and power. Look at all the trouble we get into thinking we know more than we do and acting as if we are more powerful or should be, and the contraction we undergo thinking that God is as we imagine. We impoverish God by contracting God to adumbrations of selected mental categories, mental contractions.

Here is an example of omniscience. We knew—at least some of us knew, or thought they knew, or simply made believe they knew—that Saddam Hussein had weapons of mass destruction and we had better get him before he gets us. Omniscience has many variations. We should know better. At times, we attribute omniscience to God and blame him for the mess we are in. We shift the blame, the cause, the responsibility. But we do not know better, and blaming does not help. It is best to acknowledge this dangerous, at times perverse quality we have, that we think we know more than we do.

Luria and Boehme tell us God contracts to make room for us. God models something for us. We need to contract, to make room. If we are only expanding, there is no room for others. It is good to be expansive and enjoy your expansive self. But if someone is telling you something deeply meaningful, something real and true and delicate for them, and you can only expand, how will you hear them, how will you let them in?

God contracted and made room for us. Not a hell of a lot of room, perhaps, but here we are, such as we manage to be. I would like to share a vision, a paradoxical impossibility, which inner vision proposes as deep reality. God is wholly everywhere. Yet we are, we exist. Can we say we exist inside God, outside God, both, elsewhere? Is there any space that is not godspace? If God is everywhere, how can we feel without Him? Yet we do. We have no access to God who is always accessible; accessible yet withdraws and, in coming and going, quickens us with pain and joy: partly a cruel vision, partly embracing. A primordial "now you see him, now you don't", connecting with the coming and going of our own aliveness and self-feeling, our emotional fluctuations. At the same time, Chassidus (Schneerson, 1998) tells us, there is a soul point ever in contact with God that, in our experience, waxes and wanes, or perhaps is like a constant hum in the background.

In Rabbi Luria's story, even though God tried to make room for us, something went wrong. Vessels that were meant to hold and transmit and transmute godly energy shattered. Vessels emanating creation broke at lower levels of formation. They could not take the intensity of the energy they were mediating. Some of the higher channels remained intact, but those most involved in what turned out to be our world (and us) shattered. I was touched in a recent Anselm Kiefer exhibit by a sculptural representation of the Shekinah in tatters, torn, smudged, burn marks on her rag-like, princess-like garment, perhaps a wedding gown (the Sabbath bride). Shekinah, whatever else, is God's Presence in us, on earth, in the tenth *Sephirot*, Malkut, one of the shattered spheres, dimensions, vessels, channels. (Appendix 1: *Ein Sof* and the *Sephirot* Tree of Life.) It is said our challenge, our job, is to repair the rupture. Wherever we are, embedded in the shatter, in the shards, the brokenness, there are divine sparks awaiting redemption with our help. And we are helped by the Divine Presence, the Shekinah, which, in Kiefer's vision, partakes in the dust and ashes of our scarred beings. One cannot help turning letters around, wondering about scarred—scared—sacred.

That creation and the creative process could not bear its own intensity teaches us, as psychotherapists, to go slow, dose it out. Wilfred Bion (1970; Eigen, 1998) sees catastrophic processes at the beginning of psychic life and writes of a sense of catastrophe as a link that cements personality together. He cites Rabbi Luria as resonant with his concerns and adds a new turn. Bion feels we cannot take the intensity of our own experience. We are, in some sense, embryonic with regard to ability to work with our experiential capacity. We are able to process or digest very little of what has impacts on us. Bion presents this as a kind of developmental and evolutionary challenge: how to grow psychic capacity to work with the psyche. Or, to put it slightly differently, how to grow ability to work with emotional problems, the disturbances human personality presents. I hope time will allow us to develop this theme further.

Bion is parallel to Luria: our system cannot take very much of itself. Experiencing cannot take too much experiencing. We do not know what to do with ourselves and our experiential capacity. The latter produces experiences that are too much for us, that we cannot "handle". If one meets this situation, begins taking it in, a broader attitude develops. If the patient seems not to be changing and you are getting impatient and irritated, contract, make room for apparent unchanging. Armed with Luria–Bion, you are aware that our system cannot take too much. Changes of energy, shifts of being and ways of being might be too much for this patient now. The patient's "unchanging" might be too much for you now. Contract, make room, for the patient and yourself, your frustration and the patient's slow pace. There are always other ways to view a situation. Much that happens imperceptibly may surface in surprising ways when one least expects it.

Remember Luria's story: God contracted all at once to create our world and life, and the vessels transmitting being could not take the process. This is akin to saying the psyche cannot take the forces of psychotherapeutic change. In psychotherapy, slow is important, dosing is important. It is not just repetition. It is giving time for someone to get ready, build capacity for a little more. Therapeutic change is difficult and it takes time to build ability to make use of it, let it happen, digest it. We have to build resources that make therapeutic change possible. Building up resources is crucial.

Some of you heard me tell this story before (at the end of *Psychic Deadness*, 1996). Susan Deri used to talk about it at meetings. It was a case of a "chronic schizophrenic" man. Over the course of fifteen or twenty years of work together, he improved. He now had an apartment; he now took care of himself. He had a more independent existence. He was alone, but he was surviving, living the life he could.

Then this man gets the idea—it came to him—that he wants to fall in love. And, lo and behold, it happens. Susan was wary about it. How could this happen, how could he manage it? Is he equipped for it? She followed him, went with him, supported him. He falls in love. And, lo and behold, someone falls in love with him. And they get married. And he's overjoyed. And he drowns on his honeymoon. He had a heart attack and died on his honeymoon. Now this love that he had, this moment of falling in love, was something that Susan did not have. She had grown children but this kind of love was not part of her life. Her patient had it but he did not have the resources to take it.

What can you say? Would it have been better for him to remain "chronic schizophrenic" (his diagnosis in those days), making do with the existence he could take, or break through his walls and shatter? Well, in day-to-day life, you usually do not have to make decisions like this. The work is slow enough and gradually you build a floor, you build resources to support feelings. Feelings need support and you build psychic resources to support the life of feelings a little at a time. Therapy supports the slow growth of affective life.

In Susan Deri's patient's case, something shattered. Vessels of life could not take the life process. Life shattered under the impact of life. How does life make room for life? In Kabbalah, God pulled back, made room, and life could not take it, it was too much, and life broke. That is a predicament we find ourselves in. We are told that our job is to repair the world, repair the vessels, put God's name together, put Humpty Dumpty back together. What does it mean to repair God's name? Help a broken God? Help a broken God within ourselves? We have severed God. We are severed beings. Severed beings with a severed God. There is no end to brokenness, no end to repair. But is it simply repair, or is brokenness part of creativity? We are creating life together, life is creating us—and what we call brokenness is part of it, part of creating.

What do we say is broken? Shirah Kober Zeller speaks of God's broken heart. Frances Tustin speaks of an infant's broken heart. The term "broken heart" is part of the wisdom of language. When Freud tells us that words or events can be a "blow to the face" or "stab in the heart", he does not mean it only metaphorically. Tustin and Zeller speak of a broken heart at the core of existence. Perhaps there are two hearts: broken and whole. Or one emotional heart capable of being both broken and whole. One being, many states and conditions.

How do we respond to our broken hearts, to God's broken heart? Fight? Get rid of it? Blame? Hide? Run? Grieve? Become violent to blot it out, destroy it? Is destructiveness a solution to brokenness? Do we have a solution? Are we the kind of beings that can develop to be able to work with broken states? How do we go about growing with a broken heart without doing too much damage to ourselves and each other? How do we survive ourselves and with what quality?

The Baal Shem Tov, an eighteenth century mystic credited as the founder of Hasidism, would say divine sparks are buried in brokenness and our job is to free them, unite them with Divinity. The Baal Shem Tov translates as something like "Master of the Good Name", or perhaps "A Good Master of the Divine Name". His name was Israel ben Eliezer (son of Eliezer). There are many tales of the Baal Shem Tov, an inspiriting presence.

Many Kabbalistic writings recycle the Greek distinction between *hyle* (matter) and animating spirit (*nous*), or rational intelligence. Matter is lower and "dumb". Spirit/intelligence animates it, gives it form. For Aristotle, rational intellect was the defining capacity for realised humanity. Lower–higher play a basic role in thinking about life and human capacities. Lower–higher categories and imagery permeate Kabbalistic vision and thought. This is partly modelled on the upright posture of the human body. Head above, feet below dovetails with sky above, earth below. When the Chassid prays, he ties a belt around his waist to signify an upper–lower division. He ascends in prayer, not descends to lower appetites. You would not be surprised to learn that a common problem in prayer is keeping out disturbing, lower thoughts and urges.

There is much to say about the upper–lower structure in human experience and perhaps we can come back to this (I amplify aspects of upper–lower structures of experience in *The Psychotic Core,* 1986). Now, I wish only to point out that the shattering of the vessels and scattering of divine sparks result in sparks being "buried" in matter. The higher is buried in the lower, the pure in the corrupt or base. There is, also, Biblical ground for this distinction. From dust we come and to dust and ash we go. God's inspiriting breath animates the clay (Adam) that man is made of. The Holy Spirit gives us Life.

The scattered spiritual sparks trapped in matter need to be released. Matter seems to be something of a villain in this context. The heaviness of matter holds spirit down. Spiritual sparks need to be

freed and united with their Source. The freeing of spirit from matter is a Kabbalah sub-theme, an important one. One often gets the sense that a basic battle is between spirit and matter, higher and lower, as if spirit is good and matter "bad". This can obscure a struggle in spirit itself, between different affective attitudes: for example, between cruelty and compassion. Struggle between caring and cruelty is also a thread in Kabbalah, in which one finds many threads in many contexts. A third complementary or compensating thread is a sense that our job is precisely to help the "material" world *in* the material world, with our *mitzvot* (good deeds), our care and blessings, work in the trenches, discovery and creative partnership in the holiness of everyday.

As a psychoanalytic psychologist, I reshape the spark story, shift its point of emphasis. I am not sure what to do with the matter–psyche distinction, it is so complex an issue, filled with possibilities (something I take up in *The Psychotic Core*). My variation of the story: the psyche is broken and has all sorts of buried sparks, sparks of life. When sparks of life come up, you think, "O my God, I'm alive!" And then it fades and you think, "Here I am again, plain me." States shift and sometimes we feel freer, a spark of life freeing a fuller, more alive, richer self. Aliveness can be many things, quiet aliveness, stillness, from the aliveness of sleeping to banging cymbals and dancing with joy (for the deep aliveness of stillness, see "The Yosemite God" in *Feeling Matters* (Eigen, 2006)). To learn how to be alive is a work in progress, touching capacities with unknown possibilities and nuances of experiencing.

I have heard Rebbe Menachem Schneerson say, "Wherever you find yourself, no matter how desolate or meaningless a place, there is work to be done, sparks to be freed." I might add, sparks to be mined. Wherever you are, there are sparks to be mined. Sparks of life to be released in whatever place you find yourself, sparks to be experienced, worked with, created—transformative moments. Sparks to contact, connect with, undo dissociations, splits. There is a hidden spark everywhere. Wherever you are means "psychically", the "place" you are living your life, the feel of your life. Whatever your psychic space might be—despair, rage, love, hate, deadness, fear, joy—wherever you are, a spark is waiting for you, for you alone, because only you can contact, distil, release, explore, and be a vehicle for your unique set of sparks. Sparks right now in a process of creation. No one can do it but you, because the sparks you are involved with are creating your own being, coming into existence with your own life. There is a saying in Judaism that the whole world, the whole creation was made just for you. Of course, that is balanced by other sayings, and by life itself. When I read the word "metta" that Sara (Sara Weber, one of the founders of the NYU Contemplative Studies Project) signs at the end of email communications—a Pali word meaning loving kindness . . . I forgot what I was going to say . . . maybe it will come back later . . . [It did, see p. 37.]

Audience member: It felt like you knew her spark when she writes that. That somehow it connects to something.
Response: That's not what I was thinking but I like it.
Audience member: Each of us are individual sparks, each of us alone to all of us . . .
Response: That's not what I had in mind but I like that, too.

We are the tender of the sparks. Not just the tender of the garden, but tender of the sparks in our garden. Sparks grow in our garden and gardens grow in our sparks.

Brokenness. Before going further with psychoanalysis and brokenness, I'd like to say another word on an aspect of Kabbalah. It grows from the *V'ahav'ta* (love God with all your heart and soul and might). In a very lonely time in my life, I would be in my bed late at night and out of the blue the words, "I love you," would come up. It was not addressed to anyone in particular. Was it addressed to me? From me? Something in me was saying, "I love you." One could interpret that I was saying it to me, but it did not feel that way. "I love you" welling up from loneliness, coming from beyond. "I love you" as a kind of support, a wish, a longing, but something, too, at the heart of devotion, something that just is.

I am thinking of one of my favorite Kabbalists, Rabbi Akiva. I visited his grave in Israel in Tiberias: a simple grave. You would not know that anyone great was buried in it. It was not like the great tombs in London; it was not like the pyramids. A simple stone, you can hardly see anything that it says. All alone in the desert sand. What a thrill, such a deep thrill. One story is that men were praying in a *shul* (house of prayer and learning) and a little boy was in the back. The men became aware of a glow coming from the back of the prayer house and when they investigated found a boy sitting and reciting the alphabet, aleph, bet, gimmel . . . He did not know Hebrew, he did not know the prayers. An illiterate boy who could not even say the whole alphabet, but what he knew he repeated over and over with all his heart and soul, a glow rising above him. He spoke the letters with *kavana*. Kavana can mean "concentration", "one-pointed concentration", or "intention". Some connect it with devotion, here, I feel, whole-hearted devotion. *All* my heart and soul—who can do that?!

It is good to have stories and myths. They express deep emotions of the human race or individuals, make you feel something that is real. Some touch something you feel is "all" in you, a special "all-sense" that brings wonder and tears and joy. We are only always part, and yet feel this "all".

Rabbi Akiva learned to read and write in his forties. He became, we are told, one of the great Merkabah mystics, the chariot-throne mystics. Ezekiel envisioned angels moving on four wheels, with four wings and four faces (man, lion, ox, eagle), constituting or "driving" a chariot that linked with, perhaps in some way was, God's throne. Meditating on this vision, angels, wheels, wings, chariot, faces, throne was a pure "ride" to God, the holy chariot a direct link with God's throne. Rabbi Akiva may have been an accomplished throne-chariot mystic, but much more. He died at the hands of the Romans. There were strong prohibitions imposed after the destruction of the second temple, restrictions of Jewish observance and prayer. Rabbi Akiva was killed for violating these restrictions. He was a great teacher and had a following. We are told he was crucified, perhaps burnt, but the centre of the story is, as part of the procedure, the Roman soldiers took off his skin. I picture him crucified, in flames. And while his skin was being peeled and death imminent, he is said to have thanked God for giving him a chance to know and live "m'odekha" ("might"). "All my life I loved God with all my heart and soul. I always wanted a chance to love Him with all my might. Now I can love You with all my heart and soul *and* might." "M'odekha" has various translations or meanings, *might* one of them. Possessions another—all that you possess, materially and spiritually, all that is in you, your all. Still another, to love God with both your good and evil inclinations, your all. In English, "might" resonates with power, strength, time, possibility, all that is possible, all one's being and potential.

This story touches the pinnacle of Rabbi Akiva's life, "I love you with all my heart and soul and might, everything, all I am, my all."

My very body, my very skin, my very being is now Yours in this love. The summit of the little boy reciting aleph, bet with total devotion. In a way, he was thanking the Romans for letting him know what "m'odekha" meant and helping him to realise his potential.

Be careful where spirit leads you. Dose it out. This is heavy stuff. But in some spiritual, psychological, emotional sense, most of us—I can only speak for myself—but if you are here today as spiritual seekers, then I bet it is likely that many among you were skinned in infancy.

I would like to do one more thing before we take a break. When we come back from the break we will get more into psychoanalysis. Now I would like to lead a little guided meditation. This is based on a Bal Shem Tov story. He would go to a place in the forest where he prayed. The generations after him knew the place but not the prayers. Still later generations did not even know the place. They knew there was a place and prayers, but no longer knew where or what they were. Eventually, people did not even know the forest.

I will speak and see if you can find what you can find.

Guided meditation

Picture going into the forest. You don't know where the place is. You find the place—you don't know how. Your legs, your steps were led to it. A feeling from somewhere, in your chest perhaps, some mysterious sense that is hard to pin down.

You find the place and now try to remember the prayer. The prayer that goes with the place. You can't remember it. Now think deeply, deeply listen. What prayer comes to you? Find a prayer now. If you can't find one, make one up. Let one come to you if you can, your prayer. Let it come from anywhere at all. Let it form in you, let it form you.

After finding your prayer, let it go. Remember only the feeling of the prayer. Stay with the prayer feeling. If you were to die now, is that a feeling you can die with? If not, move it around. Change it. Titrate it. Find a feeling you can die with. Feel that feeling. Let that feeling be your centre. Let it touch you. Touch it. That feeling is your life.

* * *

A short break.

* * *

There are psychoanalytic notions of brokenness—emotional nuclei—that aspects of Kabbalah and psychoanalysis share. But before getting into that, I cannot resist plucking out some phrases from the psalms. I do not know if everyone knows or reads the psalms. One of my ways of reading the Bible is to tune into the vein, the thread, the emotional world dramatised by the characters at a particular moment. If you bracket the belief system for a time, if you can do that, you are going to find sets of powerful emotions. If you do not try to name them too quickly, emotional worlds open up. The psalms are one of the quickest ways to get to some of these strong feelings.

Here are some random phrases: "My wound exudes into the night without ceasing." "My soul refuses to be comforted." "My spirit faints." "You hold fast the lids of my eyes." "I throb with pain and could not speak." "With my heart I meditate, and my spirit searches diligently." Some phrases that occur to me now have to do with depths. "Depths" is a big biblical term. Depths associated with God and associated with us: "Out of my depths I cry to you." "You search my hidden depths."

It does not take much to live your way into the feelings these human beings, who lived long ago, expressed. People writing about depths of feeling. Human depths, Godly depths.

Will my Lord, my God, cast me out forever? Will He no longer be favourable? Has His kindness ceased forever? Has His anger shut off His mercies? Does He act this way to terrify me, to bring me to Him? "Out of the depths, out of the abyss, I cry to You."

Here are a few more phrases: "Seek His presence continually." "You have put me into the lowest pit." How can you keep seeking His presence continually if He put you into the lowest pit? I think of Job: "Yay, though You *slay me, yet will I trust* You." Where does that come from? Freud's masochism, the death drive? Yay, though You *slay me, yet will I trust* You. It silences psychoanalysis. "Render justice to the lonely and the orphaned." "A burnt offering You do not desire. The offering You love is a broken spirit, a broken and humble heart." "Make me have gladness in rejoicing so that the bones You have crushed will rejoice." "In Your light do we see light." "Reflect in your hearts upon your bed and be still." "You put joy in my heart." "All who take refuge in You will sing forever." "Sing a new song unto the Lord (YHVH)." "I will sing to my God as long as I live."

There is a phrase, "holy mountain", a phrase you will come across in the sutras and psalms, where mountains dance with joy and skip. Skipping and dancing mountains are something that both Zen Buddhism and the psalms speak of. Such exultation that even mountains dance and skip and sing.

One might say there is a kind of bipolar range of emotions the psalms give us. The depths of despair without You, bereft of the Holy Presence. The beloved is gone, the Other gone. Winnicott describes a situation I call "the Z dimension". Winnicott writes of a mother who goes away from the baby for X time, then comes back and the baby is all right. Mother goes away for X + Y time, comes back, baby is all right enough, takes a hit perhaps, but weathers it. Mother's gone for X + Y + Z time, comes back, baby is changed permanently. A permanent alteration of the kind Freud speaks of in "Analysis terminable and interminable" (1937c). One might say, something of the infant is gone, has entered the Z dimension. Something happened that, if not irreparable, offers dire obstacles. In the psalms, this is given expression in the most personal way, a soul journey. Here—gone. Where are You? Where is the Presence that is always here? Where did You go? Will I ever get out of hell? Worse than hell? When presence comes back, life comes back. Joy and singing come back. "I go to bed weeping and wake up laughing."

In the psalms, it appears, the Z dimension can be reversible. The soul goes under, suffers torment, death, and returns, alive, thankful, one with Life again. A deep model for therapy and daily living, as well. I think of Freud saying that the presence of dreams gives us hope that psychotic states can be helped, since we undergo temporary psychotic moments in dreams and then awake to everyday life again. I am tempted to say, also, that the presence of psalms gives us hope that the most mangled states can be helped, for similar reasons. Dreaming consciousness, void awareness, everyday waking life—all combined and variably mixed—feed the emotionally colourful world that makes us feel alive.

One thing that Judaism contributes is an amazing range of emotionality. Your emotions, your most personal emotions, the whole rainbow, hell to heaven, your broken, crying, longing, joyous heart— I do not know any literature as personal and emotional as the biblical literature. Bion has extracted from this literature many things. One is his attraction to myths or "stories" where something bad happens. They might begin happily enough. For example, the Tower of Babel story: people work together to build a tower to heaven. What could be better? Who does not want to reach heaven? Sounds like a good thing to do, build a tower to contact God. A link from Earth to heaven, from the soul to God. Building as a co-operative activity, people working well together. For some reason, God does not take a fancy to it and destroys the tower. What seems to be a good intention, linking with God and each other, turns into a disaster. People in disarray, loss of common language, connections lost, unities lost. Diffusion spreads, fragmentation spreads. What can we draw from it?

Beware of unities? Unities are dangerous? Unities fission. Unions explode. Are we marked by explosive unions? Swings between making and breaking links? A reminder that there is always difference as well as union? Where there is union, difference asserts itself (and vice versa?).

Bion asks, what did people do to deserve this punishment? They were linking up and working together and a destructive force stops them. Bion calls attention to a destructive force in human life. God plays the role of punisher in the story. But the destructive tendency is part of our beings, whether directed outside or inside. God expresses a human tendency. A configuration we know well, but find it hard to take in and work with. We make a creative, co-operative effort and something jams it, threatens to undo or deform it. In vernacular, we often say we "screwed up", "messed up". We make a linking effort and it gets damaged or destroyed. I think of the imp peering out of a man's chest on the book cover of George Groddeck's *Book of the It*. During the Second World War, unexplained mess-ups were attributed to an imp, Kilroy, "Kilroy was here."

(Digression: whimsical word play—the name, Kilroy links with Kill-*roi*, kill the king. That is, we are not masters (kings) of our own house, but subject to slippage, uncertainty, fallible reversals of all sorts, including impish destruction.)

Perhaps one aspect of destructive urges is a need to be free of links. I want to link up, but not be too linked up. I want to breathe freely, neither too linked nor unlinked. Links begin to sound like chains, and no chains like nothing. Between claustrophobia and agoraphobia, philobat–ocnophil (Balint, 1959). What do we do with this paradoxical, double capacity? I call it a distinction–union structure, a double or paradoxical structure, in which distinction and union tendencies contribute (Eigen, 1986, 1992, 1993, 1995, 2011). Each of these threads or tendencies, distinction and union, has a biography.

Some people are more one or the other. A union person might be afraid of distinction. A distinction person might be afraid of union. Whichever side is dominant, the other side will manifest itself. Many movies portray dramas between distinction–union tendencies. Different characters portray different tendencies. You might have a very separate type of person and a very union type of person. By the time the movie ends, each has made a little move towards the middle or the relationship explodes or collapses. Both tendencies can be explosive or dictatorial, validating one capacity over the other, veering between collision and elusive dissociations.

The Babel story has both of these tendencies. At the outset, we are united, co-operative. We build, then destroy. A destructive force comes. Probably from within and between ourselves, the friction of differences or suffocation of claustrophobia breaks the unity.

Cosmic thinking tells us there are destructive forces in the universe. And, since we are part of the universe, destruction works through us. There are creative forces in the universe, destruction part of the mix. We do not know what to make of relationships between creativeness–destructiveness. Bion calls attention to a conjunction of tendencies: we build, unite, work together, and destroy what we are building at the same time. I used to see Con Edison (a utility company that supplies electricity) signs when workers were destroying the streets: "Dig we must for growing New York."

One of my favourite quotes about the universe, by the physicist, Eddington: "Something unknown is doing we don't know what." Something unknown. Do I hear *Ein Sof*? The unknown infinite of infinites, for which there is no name or knowledge, our unknowing the only means of approach? How does unknowing and something unknown fly in the face of omniscient, omnipotent us? Unknowing meets our know-it-all attitude. Know-nothing, know-everything, and something in between.

I used to worry during the Cold War that the United States or Russia would press the atomic war "button" from the viewpoint of omniscience. One or the other side would falsely think it knew something about the other that, in fact, it did not know. For example, "knowing" Russia was about to press the button so we must press the button first. Well, thank God that did not happen. But a version of it happened in Iraq. A sense or pretence that we knew something about Iraq that we did not, imagining Saddam Hussein to possess weapons of mass destruction that threatened us. And it continues. Psychopathic use of omniscience to get what one wants. Psychopathic use of omniscience and phony omnipotence. We, protector of democracy, also a bully, the strongest, Number One, the most powerful nation in world history, etc. So much that we attribute to God in some way applies to our own states and attitudes. Omniscience and omnipotence, for example. Apply these to yourselves. How does omniscience–omnipotence work in your own life? How has it helped you get as far as you have? How does megalomania play a role in creativity? How does it help? How does it mess things up? We all have to pretend to know more and be stronger (and maybe weaker too) than we are to get through childhood, even to get through our daily tasks.

Bion draws out mixtures of tendencies in biblical stories like Eden and Babel. Curiosity, good fruit, desire, wanting to be like God, something bad happens. Desire–punishment, or, in William Blake's terms, innocence–experience. Good turning bad is a basic structure Lurianic Kabbalah and Bionic psychoanalysis share. Both gravitate to catastrophic realities. Bion shadows Lurianic Kabbalah by depicting trauma and psychic origins with a Big Bang image, a constitutive psychic shattering. He relates the Big Bang image to an explosive beginning of psychic life and also the birth of psychosis (Bion, 1970, Chapter Two; Eigen, 1998, Chapter Three). In psychosis, he depicts an explosion (trauma), with bits and pieces of personality floating in space at accelerating velocity, going further and further away from each other and further from the point of explosion (O, origin). Links thin, possibly are lost as diffusion grows. Catastrophe links personality together. Some of these bits and pieces might pop up and hit you in the therapy room, and you might try to talk about them and make sense of them. But you might be running before you have a ball. The bits and pieces of exploded personality floating in the room might not be redolent with meaning so much as flotsam and jetsam of an extended SOS signal, like a thinning, vanishing scream over time (Eigen, 2002, pp. 151–155). You might be speaking to the wind as the piece you address continues to rush away. It just happened to pass through your office at that moment. Even so, the vanishing debris might have value as passing signals of a catastrophic process that began long ago and still goes on.

A therapeutic value of this depiction is support in keeping your eye on the originating explosive process. Feel the impact, an implicit sense that might be translated something like:

> I am a catastrophe in process. My personality is catastrophic. Something awful has happened, is happening. I am undergoing a state of disintegration, flying off into space. I am happening to me; I am a constant disturbance to myself.

A black box, a black hole is flashing an extended SOS signal. It is signalling that there is no end to destruction. If you are getting frustrated because the patient is not getting better, maybe you are trying too hard or working with something that is unavailable. Maybe part of what needs to happen is to sit with the explosion, hear the SOS.

A Kabbalistic exercise, suggested by Rabbi Nachman is: listen, hear the scream. There is a scream inside. It is faint, dying out, perhaps already has died out. But when you listen, it gets louder and louder. Stay with that scream, an inaudible scream of your patient's being, perhaps your own being as well.

What do you do with a screaming adult, a screaming baby? The scream is a sign of distress that cannot be addressed by the screaming one. A distress the adult or baby cannot solve, an unsolvable disturbance. And that is where you come in. Not that you have a quick fix, a solution. But you are prepared to stay with that scream for decades, to sit with the unsolvable disturbance, providing a background. A background support for something to grow over time.

So catastrophe, explosiveness—a big theme in Bion and Kabbalah. The shattering of the vessels, the shattering of personality. What can the psychoanalyst bring in face of this catastrophic happening and ongoing disturbance?

Bion called psychoanalysis—for example, the psychoanalysis that he underwent with Melanie Klein—a catastrophe. He speaks of psychoanalysis as a catastrophe one has to survive.

What is the state, the attitude, he counters to catastrophe? For Bion, the attitude, state, and disposition with which we meet catastrophe is Faith. Not "K", not knowledge. He is not anti-knowledge. Knowing plays an important role in his work. But it is faith he posits as the only state of being that meets catastrophe (Eigen, 1993, Chapters Eleven and Seventeen). He creates a special notation to express this: F in O, where O signifies unknown ultimate reality, especially, in psychoanalysis, emotional reality. He calls Faith the psychoanalytic attitude, which includes the discipline of being without memory, expectation, understanding, or desire. Paradox: psychoanalysis as catastrophic, the psychoanalytic attitude (F) the way to meet it.

Something in Bion's work touches a chord in Saint Augustine's *Confessions*. You go through everything with Augustine. He becomes obsessive. Should I go to a play? Have sex with my girlfriend? I am not fully devoted to God if I go to plays and have sex. He loved plays, loved his girlfriend, but felt Eros and theatre conflicted with his love for God. In each chapter he goes through gruelling conflict. He exercises thought, but will fails. Reason is not enough, but he takes it as far as he can. There is spiritual suspense, human suspense. You do not know what is going to happen at the beginning of a chapter. You might "know" cognitively, but Augustine takes you through it emotionally. You are in emotional suspense and crises. All his knowledge seems helpless in the face of obsessive difficulties. Helpful to a point, then a limit. The chapters end with reason trailing into Faith, into love: O my God, I love You. You are wherever I am. You are in my anxiety, my inability to help myself, in my abyss; You are in my unsolvable problems, my unsolvability. Wherever I find myself, You are there. Every chapter ends like that. Augustine finds God everywhere. Wherever he is, God is. A little reminiscent of the culmination of Job's mystical moment—just God! Faith itself.

For Bion, the psychoanalytic attitude is Faith. Most workers associate psychoanalysis with knowledge, understanding, insight (K). Many Bion readers emphasise K. But, as Bion's work unfolds, F assumes central importance. In my writings on the area of faith in Bion (1993, 1998), I try to work out relations between faith and knowledge, an ongoing effort. A certain primacy of faith emerges that situates knowing. Grotstein (2007) is one of the few who sees this aspect of Bion's work and amplifies it (e.g., his writings on the background subject or Presence of primary identification). Bion emphasizses what is not known in a session. A session is about what we do not know. We work with unknown impacts. Faith is an opening to the unknown.

What on earth can faith do in face of catastrophic realities, big bangs, small bangs, explosiveness, shatter, shards, sparks? For Bion, in faith we do not know, but its call to openness does something to *us*. I go back to a moment in Job's story: "Yea though You slay me yet will I trust You". A moment of Bionic faith. A process of transformation Job unwittingly lived, peeling layers of perception, mystical skin.

Bion denotes unknown reality as "O" and writes of Faith in O. O can be catastrophic. It gives rise to many kinds of impacts. The *Song of Songs* registers O-impacts in another key, in terms of erotic longing and bliss rather than imminent catastrophe. In a sense, O is Eddington's unknown doing we don't know what. We can make a case that O resonates with *Ein Sof* in its unknowability. In a deep and pregnant sense, Bion is a guardian of the unknown.

In *Cogitations* (1994b, pp. 323, 325; Appendix 4: O-grams), he offers two O-grams (my term), a kind of tree of life, starting with O alone at the bottom, giving rise to cosmic–human creative ventures, offspring. In a way, Bion's depiction complements the Kabbalah tree of life (the *sephirot*), which starts at the top and flows downward, *Ein Sof* beyond the top, above the *sephirot* channelling downward flowing divine life. (Appendix 1: *Ein Sof* and the *Sephirot* Tree of Life.) Bion's second O-gram (1994b, p. 325; Appendix 4, O-gram No. 2) has arrows pointing downward from all the creative offspring towards O, which stands alone at the bottom. Taking the two O-grams together, we can envision creative flow bottom up, top down, or in all directions. What we learn or discover or create at "higher" levels feeds back to O, interacts with O, generating further creativeness.

While energy emanates top-down in the *sephirot* and bottom up in Bion's O-gram, there is multi-directional flow of possibilities. Marion Milner is fond of pointing out that energy flows both ways, top–bottom, bottom–top. This, too, is inherent in Bion's and Kabbalah's depictions, above ↔ below. But a difference in representations exists which must be pointed out: O at the bottom, *Ein Sof* at the top.

The O-grams suggest a profound monism; O-transformations at work in the creative fanning of life through experience and its expressions. Bion writes that he is interested in the poetry of life, the poetic spirit, yet the roots of poetry are in language. And language? He asks, "What is important? The root? The flower? The germ? The conflict? The durability?" (1994b, p. 323; Appendix 4) He adds that any other experiential domain can be substituted for categories he chose. Sight can be "replaced by taste, touch, smell, sound, etc., from infra-sensual to ultra-sensual" (p. 325). Bion leaves open how one might depict the particular experiential domain constituted by psychoanalysis. Perhaps it would have roots and branches or, as some might say, grow more like a rhizome. Bion's grid (1994b, p. 295; Appendix 5) might be one attempt at representing aspects of a psychoanalytic domain, but expressive attempts are very much in process. Whatever representations you favour, for Bion, psychoanalytic experience invites exploration in its own right.

Whether *Ein Sof* at the top or O at the bottom, Bion protects the unknown, and Faith for him is an attitude of approach to the unknown: a radical faith in the face of decimation. He even speaks about suffering joy, building capacity to suffer joy. It could be assumed that joy is easy to take. But, from the perspective Bion develops, our capacity to bear and process any affective state is lacking. Care, development, and time is needed to begin the kind of growth of capacity needed to digest emotional life and see where it can go. When he writes that every dream is an aborted dream, he means that every affect is an aborted affect—partially aborted. He writes as if the affective world is difficult to take, that we cannot tolerate and do not know what to do with our feelings. Often we break off what we are experiencing, divert, escape, re-channel, act out, somatise, and engage in creative struggle. Our psychophysical system produces states it cannot process, its productions ahead of ability to digest and use them. In extreme instances, our own impact on ourselves can kill us or make us sick. We sometimes fall ill, even die, from intensity or strangeness of feelings, at times at a loss for a frame of reference for experience. In one of his images, Bion suggests as analogue, bleeding to death in our own tissues. At any moment, our K functions might not be up to the task of understanding what is happening to us, including our own effect on ourselves. And yet, how precious are moments of realisation, seeing an experience through as best we can, the unexpected unfolding of life as we grapple with it, as we wait on it.

I recently received a report on Internet mailing lists detailing the progress research on schizophrenia has made, emphasising neural imaging and chemical treatments. Yet, the report ended by saying that we cannot rely on the very biological interventions it praised, for example, that there is nothing we can find in neuro-imaging that tells us what do with a psychotic individual in real life. There are too many complexities, gaps, and possibilities at work. We get back to some unknown place. We experiment with medications and sometimes they are very helpful. I am not anti-medication. Yet, it is good to keep in mind that there are unknown aspects to what we are medicating.

This is even true with an electric light. I can turn a light on or off, but I do not know how it works. An electrician knows. But, if you push him, "Tell more about electricity", at some point he will get to the end of his knowledge, perhaps pretty quickly. What the hell is electricity? We do a lot with a lot of things with very partial knowledge of how they work or what they are capable of doing. Scientists tell us most matter of the universe is unknown, we do not know what it is. If this is true of the physical universe, whatever we mean by physical, how much more so with the psychical and spiritual. We know how to push and pull some switches, but what we are pushing and pulling remains a mystery.

We can have a good meditation session and open a channel. But what are we monkeying with? We might depict faith as an intuitive organ, an attitude through which we try to meet what we monkey with: faith as an open channel in face of everything. Or whatever we can take of everything. How much life can we take, our leaky, explosive, alone and together life?

Alone—all one. All one—alone. Back and forth, a kind of psychic heartbeat. Now this, now that. Building the tower of Babel, destroying it. God—no God. Self—no self. Back and forth, both together, terms of constant conjunctions, dual tendencies, capacities, states, moments.

Perhaps we are trying to develop another way of thinking, a more inclusive attitude. Not just this *vs.* that. We are not too far along this path. We fight over beliefs instead of taking beliefs as signals, bleeps of larger rhythms of which we have intimations. Buddha did not take a stand about many belief systems—is the soul eternal? What is the ultimate nature of the universe? When strong beliefs came into view, beliefs people fight over, Buddha might say, "I don't know. I can't decide. It is not relevant to you growing as a person, working on yourself. Practise. Keep practising." So many unanswerable questions. So much to do, unending work with oneself, trying to open, help instead of harm. Buddha was a little like Freud saying that free association will free you from karma. (Donald Levy, Emeritus Professor of Philosophy, Brooklyn College, suggested this to me.)

We are made of rigid, persistent systems that go through almost anything. Yet, we are also fragile. Fragile, supple, resistant, and resilient. Flexible, rigid beings. You never know what will break when. A psychological breakdown, a somatic breakdown. Psychic symptoms, somatic symptoms. So many tensions, the tension of being alive. We are unsolved problems. Our feeling of aliveness itself can be a problem with no solution. How to dose emotional life, channel aliveness. How to work and live with aliveness is an unknown we are working on, experimenting, trying.

We have touched several themes in Bion: catastrophe, faith, dosage, unknown reality, O. How much of ourselves can we take and with what quality? There are other themes we may not have time for. One is transformations. Both Kabbalah and Bion are interested in what Bion calls transformations. Transformation is part of spiritual or mystical experience from ancient times and before. Cave paintings of 32,000 years ago suggest transformative impacts. An archaeologist interviewed in Werner Herzog's film, *Cave of Forgotten Dreams*, suggests we be re-named Homo Spiritus rather than Homo Sapiens. Different approaches to transformations could be a seminar in itself.

In the first O-gram (Bion, 1994b, p. 323; Appendix 4), O transmutes to Root, which transmutes to Instrument (tools), God, Stone, Language, Paint, and these give rise to music, religion, sculpture, poetry, and painting. You can make your own O-tree, expressing the creative veins most meaningful to you. O runs through them, gives rise to all of them. Another meaning for O: One. Or Other. You might call it creative spirit. But it is nameless. The One, the many. All creative activities of humankind branching from an unknown substructure. You are an O-branch made from O-processes. A paradoxical conjunction or synchrony of One and Other.

In the second O-gram (Bion, 1994b, p. 325; Appendix 4), O gives rise to Godhead and Analogues, which give rise to beta elements, which give rise to alpha elements, which give rise to pictorial image and representation, which give rise to horse and ideogram. All of these processes point back, flow back to O.

Between image and thing in itself, Bion posits unknown alpha function, a meaningless term to note something happening that transforms perception through image to elemental naming. He calls name a hypothesis that bring things together. We are already thinking, feeling, sensing on the road to more thinking, feeling, sensing. Emotional experiences are expressed in myths and dreams, at once ideograms and narratives, with more abstract transformations ahead (see Bion's grid, 1994b, p. 295 and Appendix 5: Bion's Grid).

Meditation on Bion's O-grams opens rich fields to explore, emanating from unknown reality (Kabbalah: *Ein Sof*). For psychoanalysis, unknown emotional reality, which Bion describes as infinity: "The fundamental reality is 'infinity', the unknown, the situation for which there is no language—not even one borrowed by the artist or the religious—which gets anywhere near to describing it" (1994b, p. 372).

How does psychoanalysis, which we are repeatedly told is a verbal therapy, touch the infinite unknown, wordless reality? All kinds of unknown emotional transmissions occur during therapy. You do not have to be talking for them to occur. Your supportive presence, background atmosphere, tone, and texture has an impact over time that might be more important than anything you say. The combination of word and atmosphere are part of the soup, part of the ingredients. But Bion holds fast to the predicament that the basic reality we work with, partner, is unknown infinity: we nibble bits and pieces of unknown infinite emotional reality. It is freeing to feel we are nibblers, sometimes gulpers. Always qualified by more nibbles. We make our declarations, have our beliefs and convictions. We say you are this; you are that. We use the *DSM* for insurance companies and partly for education. But our declarations, beliefs, and categories are pimples of a deep emotional pull or presence that has no beginning or end and we do not know where we are in relation to "it". We put ourselves at "its" disposal.

Let me sum up some of overlapping themes in Bion and Kabbalah: catastrophe, Faith, intensity of affect, shatter, and transformation. Bion's grid and O-grams are like inversions of the sefirot. If we had time, we could go into the *sefirot* and Bion's grid and O-grams and see how they relate. They are kind of upside down with each other, so to speak. But the *sefirot* are all interrelated and all the parts of Bion's grid and O-grams are interrelated. You can move upside down, downside up, side to side and find intricate transformations and blends. Something like the children's song: Hashem is here, Hashem is there, Hashem is truly everywhere; up, down, all around, that's where He can be found. (Hashem—The name, meaning God). There are apparently directional flows at a given moment, but if one looks closely one finds swirls, other flows, multi-directional, everywhere at once. Maybe this omni-directionality is part of what makes people paranoid.

In the time we have left, I would like to mention other aspects of psychoanalysis that resonate with the theme of shattering. In Winnicott's (1992, Chapter Thirty-Four; Eigen, 1993, Chapter Eleven) "use of the object" portrayal, he depicts the baby destroying the mother in fantasy. In a destructive fit, the baby is in danger of mentally destroying the other. For Winnicott, much hinges on the outcome of this drama. In the best outcome, Winnicott envisions the mother surviving the baby's attacks in a non-retaliatory way, maintaining her integrity as a person and not reactively collapsing. She survives destruction intact, without falling apart, or diminishment, or inducing guilt. The mother goes through the experience with the baby, coming through in a good enough way. This leads to the baby experiencing a fresh sense of otherness. The other is beyond his omnipotent control, is real, and this realness is nourishing and can be used for growth purposes.

Not all outcomes are so optimal. We are all not as good as Winnicott's mother. We deform, go blank, fall apart, get angry, afraid, helpless, vanish, self-erase, or disappear. I might not be too good at surviving destruction in a particular moment. Sometimes, I cannot take very much and withdraw or freeze or go into hiding for a while, or say something uncalled for. But, in time, I regroup and come back. You might say I survive the patient's destruction over time, if not at a particular moment. I have gradually learnt to live my way into the fact that I might not be able to take very much, that attention comes and goes. Sometimes, a patient thinks I am looking at the clock when I might be fading out, staring around. But I do come back. Hello, I'm back! Sometimes, when someone catches on to me, she can see—oh, he's back. If patients survive me long enough, they learn to cut me slack. They can get mad or express what they feel, knowing that I come and go. We have to learn to cut each other slack if we are going to survive each other. I do come back. That is our job. We can do that. We keep re-forming, re-shaping (Eigen, 1995).

Meltzer (Meltzer, Hoxter, Bremner, & Weddell, 2008) described what he called dismantling of attention in autistic children. Something hurtful happens and they are "gone". Where do they go when they are gone? Meltzer felt he linked an autistic child's coming and going with separation anxiety: for example, the analyst's forthcoming vacation, a break in therapy, or other threat of leaving. Threat of breaking the link between child and therapist transforms into stopping mind.

Fear of the analyst's leaving could precipitate "gone" states in the child. It is hard to believe this is always so, but, even if it is sometimes or often so, a link is made between threat and dismantling of attention, "gone" states. When threatened severely enough, mind disappears, goes blank, numbs, vanishes. My experience is that mind working overtime is also a response to emotional pain or threat of pain (in psychotic states threat is reality). Mind speeds up, becomes hyper-vigilant, as if searching for an answer, racing to find a way out. Speeding turns into fading away; racing—gone. Some autistic children spin round and round as fast as they can. "Normal" children do this, too. But, in autism, you feel something more desperate. You feel the mind whirring, then stopping. Children who spin might be enjoying an altered state, a different form of consciousness, for a moment transcending ordinary painful consciousness, shedding mental skin, stopping life's anxieties, dissolving boundaries and frustration. Perhaps these are some reasons why spinning tops are so fascinating.

Meltzer's link of separation anxiety with "gone" states resonates with Fliess's (1973) depiction of going blank when traumatic memory threatens to appear, blankness as response to trauma. We find ways to dismantle attention in face of psychic threat. While it is important to be able to link threat and loss of attention, much of the time the coming and going of states seem more chaotic and haphazard. Often, you do not have a clue. Often, you come and go in sessions, and sometimes you can make a link with how the patient is affecting you or threats coming from your own internal states. At the same time, it can be fruitful to have a sense of how your coming and going affects the patient. Psychic threats go both ways. An important part of therapy is living through mutual threats, absences, breaks in contact and hyper-infusions of contact. One of our great strengths, a virtue, is that we do, a good portion of the time, come back, whether it takes a week, a month, a year, or a minute. We're gone, we come back. We're hurt, we recuperate. That is a rhythm we unconsciously model for the patient. They, too, break, come back.

Winnicott (1992, Chapter Twenty-One; Eigen, 2004, Chapter Two) writes of going through a kind of breakdown and recovery in sessions. The analyst does something that is experienced as traumatic, and the patient undergoes temporary breakdown. By the session's end, or some point in therapy, spontaneous recovery occurs. A rhythm of pain and recovery. Winnicott feels that in such moments we dip into mad states, disorganised states, and learn to come through them better. Therapy, in a way, is practice in going mad and being the better for it. Such moments can be precipitated unwittingly by the therapist, for example, saying the wrong thing, being misattuned without knowing it, not being there.

Winnicott told me of one such moment. A patient he had been working with for some time wanted to centre his image in her handheld mirror. He was behind her, and as she tried to centre his image he could see it was off centre. He moved to help her get his image in the centre of the mirror and knew immediately he made a mistake. The next time she came to see him she said, "You know, if that happened six months ago, I'd be back in the hospital." She had been in and out of hospital and they were working on fragile areas of personality. Enough had been done for the patient to tolerate mistakes. It is important to be able to tolerate being off-balance. Who is balanced anyway?

Perhaps this woman's mother could not tolerate off-balance moments that are part of raising a child. Perhaps she needed to be the centre of her child's life. Was Winnicott's patient testing him, seeing if he could tolerate not being her centre, if he could tolerate her keeping him off balance? Such moments are often paradoxical, touching different tendencies simultaneously. Sometimes we need to tolerate being the centre; sometimes we need to tolerate being off-centre, or, as Woody Allen portrays in one of his movies, "out of focus". In focus, out of focus, in centre, off centre.

Back to use of object, where the other is potentially thrown off by the baby's destructive fantasies, yet somehow comes back, reforms, survives, works with it, takes it in, thinks about it—all this mostly unconsciously, distilled in a spontaneous feeling response. A rhythm of impact–response. This paradigm can be applied to many situations and interactions: baby–mother, patient–therapist, political interactions, interactions between intimate partners. Clare Winnicott (personal communication) felt it described an important part of her and D. W. Winnicott's marriage, how they lived. I would like to add what seems to me a useful qualifying knot. It might be that a mother's or partner's or therapist's response is off, a lot or a little, but then one adjusts one's response, comes a little closer to getting it "right", or better, or good enough. There are variations in how we respond to each other's destructive urges, fantasies and expressions of the latter. Sometimes, we are better than others. Sometimes, we "get it", sense the communication, feel what is off and respond well. At other times, we miss the boat, whether from incapacity, fatigue, or our own reactive tendencies and destructive needs. The mother tries this, that, a response does not work, still trying, a response works a little better, then a little better still. At last, the baby stops crying. I must have done something right, good enough.

What is at stake is more than thinking the baby is hungry when it is wet, or wet when it is chilly, and the like. This is not about hunger or nappy or thermal states, although it could be. It is about feeling states, attitudes, and disposition. I feel x and she thinks I feel y. I feel frightened and she thinks I am happy. I am furious—can she bear my intensity? Can mother survive me and with what quality? Can we survive each other? Can we survive ourselves—can we survive our own feeling life—and with what quality?

Winnicott's emphasis is on the other surviving my destructive feelings. If you are in a partnership with someone—a marriage, a deep relationship—you are going to have to learn how to survive each other's destruction of you. Surviving destruction is a key, essential to a relationship surviving. The quality with which you survive each other's destructive needs is a key to the quality and evolution of the relationship. I remember André Green saying every relationship is conflicted—the only question is, does the conflict lead to growth or not? Bion and Winnicott touch a core issue, destructive urges as part of relationships. Perhaps destructive urges and potential impacts are part of every relationship. Is it destruction that can be survived with a quality that makes life worthwhile and enables growth?

To complement Winnicott, who writes of the other surviving my destructive urges, Bion (1994b, p. 104; Eigen, 2004, Chapter Two) writes of my getting murdered and being all right. Being murdered by the other and being all right. That might not be an easy place to get to, but it is not an impossibility. You learn how to do it over the course of your life, sometimes better, sometimes worse. Every process has variability. How to get killed, survive destruction, and still be there for oneself and others. It is a freeing capacity to develop. It helps one be freer from oneself as well as more able with others. It is a double destruction, a double shatter Winnicott and Bion are up to: you surviving me, me surviving you. Me surviving your destruction of me, you surviving my destruction of you. I would add: me surviving me and you surviving you.

If psychoanalysis contributed nothing else to the evolution of psychic life and culture, that would be more than enough. This basic, dual tendency in relationships has never been stated in such clear, succinct, and challenging ways, with elaborative fantasies to go along with these destructive fields. It is something psychoanalysis can be proud of. No other discipline that I know has done it so well. Psychoanalysis works with these tendencies and possibilities in one-to-one relation over time, going through whatever one goes through. It is a learning that spreads, as Clare Winnicott pointed out, to the rest of one's life.

If we had time, I would relate surviving mutual murder to the *sephirot*. For example, I am talking with my wife and she says something that destroys me and I think, *gevurah* is flaring up, this can turn into a catastrophe. If I am lucky, there will be a quick flash of lightning, *chochma*, which, if channels open, runs through the tree, a redistribution of power, recentring, and in an instant, instead of becoming a monster, *chesed* comes. From a moment's fury and judgement—how dare you say this about me!—to seeing it from the other's viewpoint and saying, wow, I did not realise what an idiot I was being and now that I see it from her eyes, I see another perspective. A moment making space. (By *gevurah*, here I mean something like judgemental fury; *chochma*, a kind of wisdom flash; *chesed* as compassion, loving kindness, mercy; all of these states commingling, offsetting each other, contextualising potentially destructive reactivity and enabling growth. For a diagram and discussion of the *sephirot*, see Appendix 1: *Ein Sof* and the *Sephirot* (The Tree of Life.)

Psychoanalysis is about giving time and making space. Giving time for these processes to begin to work. They are embryonic and take time. Minute micro-processes, often invisible and inaudible, but they grow over time. You have to give them time and psychic space. In *Psychic Deadness* (1996), I wrote about a lovely woman, a fine analyst, who came for supervision. Her patient was suicidal and getting worse. As we talked, it became clear that she could not identify with her patient's dishevelled, messy, abject state. Her patient was not put together like she was and seemed to be oblivious to her progressive deterioration, or could do nothing about it. In contrast, the therapist was mess-phobic. I had fantasies of the therapist maybe coming to work with her hair a little dishevelled, not so perfectly put together. More deeply, it became clear that if she did not let in some empathy for the mess, her patient's shame would keep escalating. Shame would kill her.

One of the findings of *Psychic Deadness* is that you can be too alive for your patient. You can be too good for your patient. Self-hate can be so huge, the mess so acute, catastrophe so bleak, that you cannot find it or let it in. Or you might be more like me and find it but do not know what to do with it. I seem to have a sensor that gravitates towards the catastrophic, the poisonous. For me, it is intuitively obvious. But how to be and what to do is another story. For my supervisee, the wrecked soul of her client might as well have been another species, another world. She would have to find a way to let down some of her perfect aliveness or this patient would die.

In *Psychic Deadness*, I write of a gradation, a continuum of aliveness–deadness. With some people you have to become "deader" for a long time. They say in Zen, be like a corpse. Or, in Kabbalah, contract, make space. Be patient, do not break the vessels. Or, if they break, be ready to work with ruptures. We are being challenged, stimulated to grow capacities to work with breakage as part of our evolutionary task. We are, over millennia, trying to learn how to work with what we break, or what breaks under the strain of life.

Modulate your aliveness to fit the requirements of where you are, who you are with. If in a quandary, one supervisor told me, "When in doubt, wait it out." That does not always work, but in the case I was just speaking about, the therapist kept trying to "push" the patient into life, "analyse" her bad feelings about herself, encourage her. But the push and encouragement and analysis came from another plane, a "higher" plane, not the living reality of the moment, places that need touching, person to person, self to self. The term "understand" has a sense of getting under, standing under. Getting under rather than over the patient.

Psychoanalysis is very good at shaming patients, adding to the bad feeling of not being better than you are. For Freudians, it used to be "making the Oedipus". Being a "pre-Oedipal" person was more infantile, immature, undeveloped. For Kleinians, it was "making the depressive position". Moving from a more infantile, primitive paranoid–schizoid position to the "depressive", where ambivalence is tolerated and one relates more as a whole person to whole people. A kind of "moralism" creeps into most schools with higher–lower, better–worse divisions. Words like infantile and primitive become taunts. Therapy itself becomes persecutory.

For me, Winnicott and Bion open further possibilities of being with people without "judging", staying with realities of the moment. If shitty, not trying too quickly to turn shit into gold. Not being an Olympic god in the face of an anal mess. Can you "lower" yourself down, make yourself "smaller" and find the place that calls for finding now? Too often, I get a sense of therapy persecuting a person: "Why aren't you related?" "Why aren't you sexual?" "Why aren't you?" Rubbing a person's nose in what they are most ashamed of: disabilities, incapacities. This human tendency is not a monopoly of any one discipline. Marx saw it at work in the ways religions and the money machine functions. It could be widespread in education.

One of my teachers years ago, Hymen Spotnitz, warned against helping to get a depressed person undepressed too quickly. He felt a point at which suicide can come is when someone starts to feel better, then feels bad again. More important than the mood of the moment is gradual work in building resources. You can get someone to feel better, but that does not mean there are resources enough to handle a better mood. Without resources to sustain better feeling, the fall down is more acute. You have to build, through gradual give and take, the capacity to sustain ups and downs.

We can share in the pride of having workers in psychoanalysis who have made real inroads in perceiving and working with human destruction. Learning to work with destructive tendencies is imperative not only for individuals, but for survival and quality of survival of the species. There are many avenues of attempts to help. We have good social workers trying to make the world a better place. This includes social reformers and activists who try to make society more kind, less cruel. And social workers who help the lives of many in clinics and homes who are handicapped by financial disability and massive social injury. Help on many levels is needed. But, without a psychic change in humankind, social action will lack the support needed for long-term sustenance.

There is a lesson to be learnt from purist communities, semi-utopian communities that experiment with creating a better society in small terms. Most of the ones I know about cracked over time because of cracks in human nature. You cannot simply legislate or idealise rivalry, jealousy, self-centredness away. The "wild" thing, the animate thing, wreaks havoc with idealised schemes. Changing outer structures might have benefits, but without profound inner psychical change, fierce, self-centred tribal scenarios will manifest. What kind of psychical change is possible? How? Will we ever know how, or intermittently try our best, groping along, struggling with our nature. The work psychoanalysis does in the trenches might be marginal in terms of world problems, but not marginal in the world of psycho-spiritual possibilities. Attempts to learn how to work with our makeup, especially destructive needs and tendencies, are valuable explorations of human relationship. We are trying to learn something about how we destroy each other and how to survive and grow through/with destruction. Can we do it? To what extent? Even a little? And if so, will it spread? We do not know. It is an area that adds to the rebirth and renewal theme, a new twist on the theme of coming through hell: coming through one's own and each other's destructive tendencies in a better way. This, in part, is where therapy work takes us. Religious disciplines have tried to work with destructive tendencies. With what result is not clear. Mass destructions that have been part of religious rivalry are sobering facts. Many individuals have been uplifted by the spiritual dimensions religions can cultivate, but bloody aspects of warring beliefs have been blood-curdling.

Psychic work with destructive tendencies within a person-to-person therapy relationship: where can this take us? Kabbalistic exercises on aggression can be helpful at certain stages. There is the story about a man fearing his hateful urges towards someone undertaking the study of Talmud and *Zohar* to learn everything he can about aggression. He became so immersed in his studies that his wrath and destructive fears faded. Some exercises encourage a person to keep observing, staring at his anger and seeing what opens. Others say, look away, substitute joy. Some say pay more attention, some say divert yourself, find another way. But the detailed study of aggressive urges? I am not sure there has been anything quite like it before psychoanalysis, although, as Freud said, poets—and I would add, spiritual disciplines—opened and continue to open many doors.

It is nothing new to see aggression as part of our survival makeup, instrumental in mating, food gathering, territory, shelter, cross-fertilisation of war. Some see it as a kind of cleansing, clearing out the old, bringing in the new, analogous to death making room for birth. Destruction, too, can be a response to claustrophobia, an attempt to break through the confines of life, the walls of personality: destruction as response to social claustrophobia, the squeeze of "civilisation". A freeing destruction, a fantasy that if I destroy everything, I will be free. My autonomous side seeking air. Freud, Klein, Winnicott, Bion, Bowlby, Reich, and Kohut are among those who make unprecedented forays into labyrinths of destructive tendencies. If we never figure out the most creative ways to meet the destructive side of our nature, it is not a problem we are free to evade. Even digesting the possibility that we might face an unsolvable problem can open paths and vision.

Let me stop talking. Any questions, feedback, fables? When we are in the realm of Kabbalah, we are in the realm of the fabulous. Similarly, when we read many of the sutras, we are in the realm of the fabulous. All kinds of things are said about Buddha that are adult children's stories. Spirit journeys, soul journeys, mind journeys of a wonderful nature. The basic discipline in Kabbalah is how to open your heart, how to turn a heart of stone into a heart of flesh, opening channels. A basic discipline in psychoanalysis is how to support personality in life and help it face its attempt to destroy itself.

Question: If the psychoanalyst builds her vessel for herself and her client, how would you describe, Kabbalistically, how, as analysts, we can hold a certain frame, a different kind of vessel, than we can provide for our child. How do we explain that our vessel seems to have greater strength and mobility when we are in a therapeutic mode than when we are parental, or just one in a group of people trying to get in line for something?

Response: First of all, I have no explanations for anything. But there will be people better at mothering than at psychoanalysing, especially if you are a new mother. My wife continued to practise for a while, and then she started getting phone calls after our first child was born. Betty, where are you? She just tended not go to sessions, she forgot about them. And when she was in her sessions, she often was thinking about her child. Eventually she stopped practising for a while until she was able to think of both her children and her patients. So, it can work either way. We can be better with our patients than at home, or better at home than with our patients, and this can vary.

What we are talking about, in part, is psychic flexibility. You should not break your psychic blood vessels. How to avoid a psychic stroke? Building up a certain background resonance . . . *Metta*—it came back to me what I wanted to say earlier when I mentioned *metta*. I better say it before it is gone. Incidentally, Bion writes of a thought frame or rhythm involving a thought or feeling appearing one moment, disappearing the next: here, gone; on, off; God, no God; self, no self; you, no you (I explore it in *Contact With the Depths* (2011) and in the Seoul seminars).

So, *metta*. Some say the flow of loving kindness starts with you. Loving kindness starts with your own self/being or deeper than self. A kind of caring warmth for yourself that has a thawing-out effect. A thawing out that touches your life and work. Whether your bigger problem of the moment is work or home or other aspects of your life, there can be a thawing out that creates a certain resonance, diminishing of paranoia, lessening of the scream and tension states involved in silent (or not so silent) screaming.

How you reach that is individual, perhaps through meditation, prayer, or music. You need to keep finding what works for you. For me, it sometimes happens by seeing a face on the subway, someone with a certain look that opens me. With my children and patients, the thawing moment ever changes. Sometimes I'm tired; sometimes I'm open. Both Kabbalah and psychoanalysis say that there is a domain of struggle. You cannot escape having to work on yourself, sometimes holding back, sometimes opening. You develop a "body English," a spiritual body English, a sensing through which your body thaws or tightens, depending on the need of the moment.

I learnt many years ago, in the 1960s, that our bodies are much tighter than they have to be, as if they are fighting off a threat. Our sphincters are tighter than they have to be in order to function. It is as if we are living under a state of threat. When you go home to your family, threat increases. A paradoxical situation, since you think, ah, the nest, safety. Yet, the closer you are, the greater the threat. Most murders occur in the family. Work and home might provide different amalgams of threat and safety.

In my first major psychoanalysis, I complained about getting better with people in the "outside" world, but when I meet my parents, I zero out. Like the Zen master who meets the King and loses his Zen.

I meet my family and my gains in psychoanalysis crumble. My analyst said, "Your parents are the last people you'll be able to relate to. Don't worry about solving that now. Stick with growing where you can." In Buddhism, "stick with your practice now." Psychoanalysis becomes a practice. My analyst's paradoxical communication was, if you flunk with your parents, make the most of it. If you live with them or on your own, use it as raw material to learn. Your family becomes an area of practice. You try this and that, juggle the chakras, juggle the *sephirot*. You sense yourself too much this way, too much that way. You meditate, you pray, you pull back, withdraw, try again. You feel not only the impact of the other on you. Some moments you sense what the other is asking for. Where are they coming from? Why do they hurt me? What happened?

Years ago, when I was dating, I could be with a girl feeling something nice happening, and then she'd say or look or do just one bad thing to me and, almost instantaneously, I'd get physically sick. I could suddenly get sick by a glance or bad word. Not just momentarily ill, but lasting a week or two. When you are with someone thirty years, or fifteen, or five, impact multiplies. The impact of the other. I learnt through experience how vulnerable, how sensitive I could be in intimate situations, something I had to work with.

Another variation involves contrast between alone states and impact of the other. I am thinking now of a creative artist who spent hours alone painting. He could feel a rush of new realities unfolding with the movement of his hand, or plunge into an abyss when movement stalled. His mood would go up or down with the state of creativity. Yet, the highs and lows were part of his alone reality, him and the work. When he had to put his brushes down, time for dinner with family, the crash was often more than he could bear. The transition was more than difficult. Suddenly, his family life seemed so trivial, a bother that did not fit in with his creative meditative state at all. His wife and children were foreign bodies, noise, impingement. The contrast was bewildering. He wanted to escape back to his work alone, where he felt magically real. At the same time, he wanted to be with his family, to share life together. A perpetual quandary. On the one hand, why can't I stay in my meditative state forever? On the other, real life was calling. Being with other people was an incessant challenge. He had to face the challenge of learning to work with transitions and discover the possibility of softer landings.

We emphasised disaster, obstacles, difficulties. Impacts of good moments multiply, too. But even the effects of good moments partly depend on how they are used. How one relates to, and uses, experience is a challenge. Does it sound silly to say that so much of life involves getting the hang of learning to live with it? Learning to live?

I see time has run out. I wish we could go on. But I suspect we have gone through something together and perhaps the day will be a little richer for it.

CHAPTER TWO

Last time, I began by saying the essence of Kabbalah is loving God with all your heart and soul and might. The essence of Torah and the essence of Kabbalah in that respect are the same. That is the essence: love God with all your heart and soul and might. I mentioned that it sounds like a commandment. You should, you will, you have to. But it is more: you are. To love God with all you are defines you. You are this love and in relation to this love.

It is a discovery. If you make this discovery, if it happens, if it comes to you that, oh, my God, I love You with all my heart and soul and might, it is a fact. It is a fact not from the outside but from the deepest inside. Schopenhauer says music is the deepest dream of the world. You could also say this dream, this music, expresses this love.

Last time I talked about my favourite historical and also fabled rabbi, Rabbi Akiva, and I will not be saying much about him today, but we talked about his *kavannah*, his devotion, and his awareness, his feeling at the end of his life when his skin was being taken off by the Romans that at last he was able to give God everything, love God with all his might, all that was in him, all that he was. In another part in the Bible it says love God with all your heart and soul and *mind*. So, there is a change from might to mind. They are both important and it is a challenge. How can one do that? What is "all"? What would "all" be? Rabbis say with the good inclination and the bad inclination. Love God with good and evil inclinations. And what would that look like?

I counted how many intersections I could find between psychoanalysis and Kabbalah, at least the psychoanalysis I am interested in, and counted something like seventeen. It is impossible to do all of these today, but I picked a few and have a hunch that what I picked might not be for everybody, but if there are some who find it helpful, I will be very happy. One has to do with links between the *v'ahavta*— loving God with all your heart and soul and might and what that can mean, what *all of you, all of me* can mean—and the centrality of faith in Bion's work.

As I mentioned last time, Kabbalah is not one thing, more an archipelago, scattered through time, perhaps starting a couple of hundred years before the Common Era, maybe earlier. Gershom Sholem tends to see it as a form of Gnosticism. Moshe Idel feels it has independent roots in the Torah, a meditation on the inner meaning of the Torah. Different geniuses of spiritual imagination related their perceptions, insights, and stories over many years. Like crumbs in a forest, we can trace tracks through the ages of texts and presences.

Often, stories and facts were confused. For example, it was thought that the *Zohar* was written roughly around 200 CE by Shimon bar Yochai, a devoted student of Rabbi Akiva. The legend was that Shimon bar Yochai and his son hid in a cave for thirteen years, escaping Roman persecution and death. While in hiding, Shimon bar Yochai was said to have formed the basis of what became the *Zohar*, in which he is a major character. Chasidim attribute writing the *Zohar* to him, taking a main character for its author. Shimon bar Yochai is revered as a holy man and celebrated today.

Scholars track the *Zohar* to a Spanish writer, Moses de Leon (1250–1305), who authored it as an act of creative, spiritual imagination. He wrote it in a strange Aramaic under the pretence that Shimon bar Yochai was its author. A story has it that when he died, pious scholars came for the manuscript he claimed to mediate, but were greeted by his wife saying, "Here it is. He made the whole thing up." Apparently he felt his visions and reflections had a better chance of being taken seriously if he attributed them to a saint like Shimon bar Yochai.

Fact and fantasy sometimes collide. Perhaps it does not matter whether it was written in the third or thirteenth century. There is a religious tradition that Akiva transmitted an oral tradition to Shimon who passed it on, its spirit resurfacing in Maimonides in the twelfth century, Luria in sixteenth century Safed, and the Baal Shem Tov in eighteenth century Eastern Europe. From this viewpoint, Moses de Leon is seen more as a redactor than original author. Whatever the literal truth, it is not surprising that fable and fact intermix. That a thirteenth century visionary would be drawn to a third century saint as his channel or "voice" is itself worthy of study. Whatever its background, the *Zohar* (Radiance, Splendour) was written, and its impact on mystical Judaism was decisive. Luria, the Baal Shem Tov, and Rabbi Nachman were among the many who studied it, and its fecundity grew. It was an evolutionary act of the mystical mind, one of an infinity of evolutionary acts.

Last time I talked about Lurianic Kabbalah and related the shattering of the vessels to Bion's depictions of psychic catastrophe. My emphasis today is going to be a little different. My emphasis is going to be on faith, the centrality of faith, and, to make it sharper, I have picked a Chasidic descendent from the Baal Shem Tov by two generations, a great grandson, Rabbi Nachman (1772–1810) and his interlocking with the twentieth century British psychoanalyst, Wilfred Bion. We will see how they light each other up or add to each other's lights. Nachman, in one of his passages, depicted the world as a kind of *dreidel*, a spinning *dreidel*. We will see if we can reap some insight from spinning minds, spinning spirits, spinning souls.

The centrality of faith. Catastrophe is central to Bion's thinking and Lurianic Kabbalah. Bion envisions catastrophe at both the origins of personality and psychotic processes. Psychotic processes are an expression of catastrophic happenings. We, as the film *Zorba the Greek* tells us, are catastrophes in our own life. We are catastrophic beings and our sense of being a catastrophic being is often part of our most intimate feeling.

Bion writes, "When two personalities meet, an emotional storm is created. ("Making the best of a bad job" in *Clinical Seminars and Other Works*, 1994a). This sentence is attributed to Bion in 1979, the year that he died. Not everyone feels this emotional storm when meeting another person. Well-regulated people probably do not feel it, but I do not know too many of them. My guess is, if numbers are "normal", the catastrophic ones are more normal. Does it sound a little weird to think of a sense of emotional catastrophe as normal?

How do we meet emotional catastrophe? With what do we meet it? Bion answers: with Faith, capital F. For him, Faith is the psychoanalytic attitude, which he depicts as being without memory, expectation, desire, or understanding. To be without memory, expectation, desire or understanding—no one does that. It is not a possible state. But it is a direction one can aim at and it makes a difference whether one moves along this path or not. To step out of these capacities, even for an instant, is freeing.

Perhaps we are on multiple paths, one the ego as centre of the universe, another without memory, expectation, understanding, desire. Filling up, letting go, different kinds of filling and emptying. Your point of emphasis might make a difference in how you feel and look after thirty, forty, fifty years. Emphasising the faith path does not mean you are done with evil. No one is done with evil. Everyone is good and evil. But it makes a difference how you approach your nature, how you relate to it. Faith-work plays some role in mitigating egocentricity.

The first Bion formula I want to give you is F in O, Faith in O. O is a sign he uses for unknown, ultimate reality, here, unknown emotional reality. Why emotional reality? He feels emotion is a core of human life. For example, he says the core of a dream is emotional experience, and mythic narratives express and organise emotional life for the group. One of our core concerns is how life feels to us, how life tastes, a sense with varying levels of depth, from how life feels when we do or do not do something, to the scent and texture of existence.

F in O. And O is unknown. It is the same unknown that Job faced. The same unknown Job came up against, cutting everything away, possessions, attachments, loved ones, leaving nothing but encounter with God, contracting to a point of mystical vision: Oh my God—it is real, You are real. Speechless awe, silenced by awe. One moment of F in O.

Rabbi Nachman also gets carried away, hit by the intensity of experience. Seeking and meeting God often involves oscillating between megalomania and unworthiness, both fused and conflictual. Nachman felt he wanted to arouse in people an awe such as never existed before in the universe, an awe of awes never known before. Nachman felt this about many things. Sometimes, he went through a morning or day and felt, "Today I am living a day such as was never lived before." About death, the same thing: "I want to die a death such as was never died before." Nachman had very intense, magnified feeling and his feelings of unworthiness also were intense and magnified. In a significant way, life was ever fresh, ever in the process of birth.

Faith in unknown emotional reality, ultimate unknown emotional reality, never experienced quite this way before this instant, yet still unknown and beckoning, vastly unknown, inexhaustible. Bion, following Wordsworth, speaks of intimations, intimations that border on convictions and lead to belief systems. We fight over beliefs. Beliefs, too often, substitute for ongoing originary intimations. Nachman and Bion call us to get back to intimations of the unknown.

Faith is deeper than belief. Belief is a way of capturing faith, taming it, putting it in a box. Faith explodes belief. Faith feels constricted by belief. At the same time, beliefs can try to give expression to faith, lead to faith, deepen it, depending on function and use. Can you have a belief that does justice to faith?

F in O is one Bion formula. Another is T in O, where T stands for transformations that go on in O. F in O and T in O. Unknown transformations, perhaps unknowable. We sometimes think we feel or sense them, intimations, perturbations, rumbles, whispers. But we do not know what kind of transformations go on in O. Saying there are transformations in O is itself a leap, hypothesis, narrative, sensing, vision. Diverse groups of people have this inkling based on certain experiences. Buddhists talk about wordless transformations that go on outside awareness, intentionality, and conscious control. O-transformations, perhaps a sensing that something is happening and you feel some of the results. A moment opens, an intimacy, a delicacy, real and elusive, not lived before (to resonate with Rabbi Nachman). An Asian teaching is that our thoughts, feelings, images, sensations are bubbles or waves arising from an unknown sea, an unknown presence. Chuang Tzu speaks of mysterious, unknown, elusive presence linked with transformations deeper than knowing. T in O.

F in O supports T in O. Everyone say it: F in O, T in O. (The group says this several times, beginnings of a kind of mantra or chant.)

Now let me introduce a villain. In the Punch and Judy show, Punch and Judy are having a good time, and woops—out pops the devil. Bion has given the most dramatic formulation of the "negative" force that I have come across. It was waiting to be said. All the medieval talk about the devil came close but could not quite get there. William Blake, too, came close.

Freud, Klein, and Bion write of a destructive force or urge or tendency, a thread of destruction that they put tracers on. Destructiveness in the human condition. They do not dodge it. They try to see how it undergoes transformations: for example, its displacements, condensations, dissociations, projections, introjections, symbolisations, idealisations, identifications, and more. Bion maximises the stakes by positing a destructive force that goes on working after it destroys time, space, existence, and personality. This is a variation on an ancient theme, with its own particular thrust, but it joins a difficulty the human race faces: what can we do about our own destructiveness? A force that just destroys; a dedicated inclination that feeds on destruction. After everything is destroyed it feeds on the totally destroyed state. It does not stop destroying. It is an eternal state, in William Blake's sense, when he writes that all states are eternal.

Bion's statement that a destructive force never stops links with Freud saying that the push of psychic energy is constant, drive pressure is constant. The latter might not seem constant, given ebbs and flows of experience, but Freud feels there is something to be gained by supposing the pressure and stress of drives as constant. Bion envisions part of this constant push as destruction that never ends, a vision that is hard to take, but sobering and, I fear, expressive of damage we do to ourselves and each other.

I like to balance Bion's depiction of a dedicated destructive force with Buddhism's Kuan Yin. Kuan Yin is variously depicted as a Buddha or aspect of Buddha, a goddess, or a psychic or spiritual force. Kuan Yin cannot do anything but be compassionate. People pray to her for favours and when favours are granted, all she wants as reward is for people to say, thank you. Do you ever find yourself saying thank you for little things during the day? I am one of the peculiar ones who go through the day saying thank you. This happens, that happens—thank you, often to no one in particular, in my heart or a whisper. I am reminded of Melanie Klein's book, *Envy and Gratitude* (1997), in which Klein depicts an inverse relation between envy and gratitude, the former making the latter difficult, leading to further personality constriction.

We have the Kuan Yin principle, which seems allied with faith, and a force that never stops destroying: an endless meeting of destruction and compassion. What are we saying when we bring these two together or connect Bion's F in O with his writings on an incessant destructive force? Incessant faith, incessant destruction. Are we saying faith encompasses destruction, while destruction destroys faith? Are we saying we have faith in something that destroys and keeps on destroying us? That we are that destruction? That we are that faith?

Can we say O is neutral, changing, giving rise to variety, now Kuan Yin, now destructive force, mixtures, fusions, antagonisms? I think of Job again as a guide, a model, when he says, "Yay though You slay me, yet will I trust You." What kind of faith is that? Everything is taken away, nothing left, everything destroyed except one thing. If God took away everything from you except one thing, what would you want left? Yay though You destroy me, yet will I tust You.

I think of Winnicott wanting to be alive when he died, faith deeper than destruction. I want to make a double formulation: faith is deeper than destruction and destruction is deeper than faith. I want them as one thing. Faith deeper than destruction; destruction deeper than faith. There can be no faith after the Holocaust. Yet there is, faith deeper than the Holocaust, yet the Holocaust is deeper than faith. It is just the way it is, if you can find it. It is not one way, it is not the other. It is both. And maybe there are lots of different relations to each other. Maybe they are in antagonistic relations, oppositional, maybe sometimes synchronous, fused, sometimes oscillating, sometimes all together at once. Variable relations between tendencies, states, realities, and capacities.

Faith deeper than destruction, destruction deeper than faith. Nachman underwent the most severe torments and doubts with regard to his faith and, above all, a sense of distance from God. On the one hand, he felt close to God, and on the other hand, he felt far. At times, the distance was so huge that he did not see how he would ever get close again. You find such feelings in the psalms. One moment the psalmist cries, "Where are you God? You've left me and I'm in an abyss, in despair." Then a reversal: "I go to sleep crying and wake up laughing. You are back and I am happy. My soul dances, great is your faith."

Emotions rotate around God's presence or absence. You leave me and I am in despair, total torment. When will you show Your presence to me again? The time will come when You will come back and my heart will sing with joy.

I sometimes relate this to what I call Winnicott's Z dimension. When mother goes away X time, baby tolerates it. When mother goes away X + Y time, mother comes back and baby has a harder time but is still all right, although going through a number of intense emotions. When mother goes away X + Y + Z time, there is a permanent alteration of the self. When mother comes back, something does not come back in the baby, something is changed, different. An abandonment of massive proportions had catastrophic consequences. Nachman went through this over and over. He lived in the Z dimension much of his life. At the same time, he lived in Heaven. He lived a catastrophic state far from God, and a joyous state close to Him.

I do not know anyone who has not had dreams of being excluded. I am not talking about feeling excluded in your waking life, which most people in this room certainly must have felt or you would not be gravitating towards me. Everyone has had dreams of being excluded, of exile. People not wanting you, you do not belong. It is the way Nachman felt with God. I belong with God and I am excluded. God has put me away from Him.

Today, Nachman might be diagnosed bipolar but, free of such labels, he felt his emotional states were messengers, God's messengers. In Nachman's tales, like Kafka's, messages were never delivered. Layer upon layer of complexity. Emotions as undelivered messages.

Nachman lived for thirty-nine years. A short life, a lot packed into it. I do not know if Nachman ever gave up on anything the soul asked for. Emotions as undelivered would not deter him. Emotions as links, paths to the Deepest Unknown of All—faith deeper and greater than delivery. The birth experience and path—what might today be called process—was more than enough, if never enough. Never enough is more than enough. Dayenu—a moment of God is more than enough. But there are many moments, never ending moments of undelivered messages always on the way towards delivery. Kafka called his whole life an incomplete moment (Kamenetz, 2010).

Faith deeper than exile, deeper than agonised distance from God, deeper than all ills. I suspect, for Nachman, there are ways in which God in the distance, perhaps, *is* distance as well, distance so painful, so close. A hellish beauty in the soul, a poignant, piercing love.

An example of Nachman's persistence, insistence, was his trip to Israel. He went, in part, because the Baal Shem Tov did not get there. The latter felt signs he encountered on the journey boded disaster and turned back. Nachman felt he was completing the journey for his great-grandfather. Perhaps spiritual grandiosity or devotion or both, Nachman took it upon himself to make good for the Baal Shem Tov. He was always making good for souls, especially dead souls.

He could see dead souls needing help and would try to free them, raise them to heaven. He would make amends. I will not recount now all the vicissitudes of his trip to Israel, enriching in themselves, inner and outer obstacles heightened by spiritual vision and an acute sense of reality (Green, 2004). All the things he went through opened psychological and spiritual doors.

Now, I want to let you know that the first moment he set foot in Israel, he felt he could leave. He did not have to stay a second more. He felt total elation; all his problems were over. Mission accomplished.

To hear someone say, "All my problems are over" rings a bell in me. Perhaps Nachman meant his tormented distance from God was now bridged. Such wonderful moments when everything seems solved. I think of letters belonging to a World Trade Center suicide bomber, reassuring him that his heroic deed will raise him to heaven, personal torments gone forever. His problems will be over, no more disturbances, no more tormenting personality difficulties. It is quite a lure, quite a promise, all personality problems over. If one stays alive, the wheel turns, new moments arrive and difficulties reassert themselves. So, for Nachman: one foot in the Holy Land and all problems solved! I will forever be close to God, torment over. But moments, days, weeks later and another story begins, another mood, more work in the trenches.

As might be predicted, Nachman did not instantaneously leave the Holy Land and his problems were not over. He became depressed when he realised that the latter continued. He went through this sequence, in one or another way, over and over. A moment that dissolves all problems, and their depressing return with a little time. I hear this sequence in therapy. Someone goes from one love affair to another and the first moments are wonderful, everything new. The World Trade Center suicide bomber washed clean by righteous devotional destruction, the lover made fresh by love. And then crash.

Do we ever learn that we cannot get rid of the psyche and its disturbances? It appears that Nachman misdiagnosed a difficulty or was taken in by a spiritual high, forgetting, ignoring, or not caring about its trajectory. A sense that now is all and all is solved gives way, in time, to the reassertion of a fuller psychic reality.

One of the basic rug pullers Nachman obsessed about was guilt over sexuality. He was following aspects of rabbinic and kabbalistic literature, which gives a sexual interpretation to Adam and Eve eating the apple. Guilt is itself the fall, punishment in itself. To have to be guilty over sexuality expresses enormous injury. There are religious responses, rules about sexuality, ways to hallow it, what is permitted, what not, its tie to pleasure and procreation, ways to tame or channel such a gift and villain. For some, achievement of abstinence, as goal or reality, becomes a path, a necessity.

Little cupid, devil of sex. Is it really *the* primary tormentor of life or one of a number? For Nachman, it was a torment that impelled him to try to eradicate the roots of sex, so as to uproot guilt. Can it work? If goodness is a goal of sexual transcendence, lack of sexuality does not necessarily achieve it. Nature and society perform experiments. Castrated men are not necessarily beneficent. If you get rid of hormones that feed sexuality, a person still can be mean and vindictive. Bracketing sex does not solve the problems of personality. You can get rid of sex and still suffer torments, you can still be a devil haunted by devils. Getting rid of sex does not solve the problem of evil, or, in less moralistic terms, a destructive drive or urge or tendency.

The problem of personality is not solved by focusing on one thing. Sex is pretty dramatic; it certainly captures attention. But often it masks egocentricity, vainglory, and will to power. Our various tendencies play important roles, contribute to the colour, complexity, and taste of life. But they go haywire, become destructive as well as generative. For most of Freud's career, anxiety was associated with libido. Towards the end, and especially as elaborated by Melanie Klein, anxiety was associated with a destructive force Freud called a death instinct or drive. Can one uproot the latter? What would that look like?

Many of you know the story of the kabbalist who bemoaned the evil inclination. He so prayed it would be extinguished that God granted his wish and when he awoke, much that made life breathe and pulse was gone. The destructive urge, too, feeds life, is part of aliveness. And feeds guilt.

Homer begins the Western canon of literature with the word "rage" or "fury". He did not begin it with "lust". It was rage over a crime of lust, an erotic theft, one man stealing another man's woman. Rage is so often close to a total, blinding feeling. We have phrases: impotent rage, helpless rage. Rage at injustice, but also rage at our will not done, loss of control, power, not being the master. In a way, Nachman was victimised by incomplete analysis of the human condition. It is easy to focus on sex, it is so obvious. But a deep aggressive force that is partly erotic, yet partly has its own trajectory? A destructive urge at once erotic and anti-erotic?

There are aggressive pleasures and an inner bent that goes beyond pleasure, a drive to destroy everything and keep on destroying. Satan was assigned erotic and persecutory components, hating love, cursing existence. What was his will and counter-will? How close does it come to the destructive gradient Bion envisions? A destructive force that destroys itself and goes on destroying. We never hear that Satan, a personification, destroys himself. Does Bion envision a destructive force that Satan could not have imagined?

In Greek literature, hubris, in Catholicism, pride—close cousins. Bion has numerous complex formulations; one ought not to overemphasise one taken out of context. A thread that runs through his work is that our personalities are problematic. Even our consciousness is a problem. We are disturbances to ourselves. As a baby, I go in and out of consciousness. I cannot take too much consciousness. I sleep, wake, sleep, wake. Suzuki spoke of dozing, waking as an old man, not resisting dropping off, coming back. He compared his state as an old man to a baby in this regard. Of course, he kept speaking and writing in old age as well. I remember Harold Boris in his dying year writing his two best books. He could not stay awake long. He would sleep, wake and write, sleep. I once heard Elizabeth Sewell say that she knew when she was thinking because she had to go to sleep afterwards. It is hard work to support consciousness. It is hard being conscious. Some sages say we are rarely conscious. Some feel we need to work to achieve consciousness even when we are "conscious" (sometimes called "sleep-walking"). If Einstein said he thought only once in his life, where does that leave the rest of us?

Consciousness is hard to support. Bion brings out how intensity of experience is hard to support. Psychic life is hard to support. We have evolved unevenly. We evolved in such a way that we can have experiences of great intensity but lack equipment to support them. Our experiential products are ahead of ability to digest them. It is as if what our personality produces is too much for us. Our experiential capacity is too much for us, too much for itself. We lag behind experiential possibilities. Freud says we die from our conflicted character wearing us down. From Bion's perspective, it is more that we lack equipment to support the amazing capacities we have. Such support, if it is desirable or possible, requires further evolution.

As of now, we cannot take too much of ourselves and, as a result, evacuate ourselves in all kinds of ways. We use ourselves creatively on the one hand, but also try to get rid of ourselves, as if the pain of aliveness is too much. Scott (1975) wrote about a conflict between waking and sleeping. A tension that applies, also, to living and dying, reflected in ebbs and flows of more and less aliveness through a day or lifetime, moments of realisation punctuated by taking time out from oneself.

The problem of lacking sufficient support for our experiential capacity marks a more general difficulty than pinning our problems on sex or aggression, although the latter are not problem free. We need to meditate on our insufficiency in the face of our own capacities rather than blame one or another of the latter for our problems. Blaming sex and aggression distracts us from the unevenness of our evolution, our not knowing what to do with ourselves. We seem to have a blaming propensity that is contagious: it is your fault, it is my fault, it is its fault, assigning simplified causality when situations are imponderably complex and tangled. Maybe it is just us and our particular unevenness of evolution that we cannot take too much of. We have to learn how to partner ourselves, even if it takes thousands of years. Maybe we should stop thinking in terms of trying to pin the tail on the donkey and try to work with the system as a whole.

Let me retell a tale from Kafka. It is about a man seeking the law. He meets a doorkeeper who refuses him admittance. The man wonders if he can go in anyway, but is told that even if he succeeds, he will meet worse doorkeepers. The man exhausts his powers, but cannot gain access. Finally, his vision darkens. Is he dying? Is it really growing dark? Yet, as it grows dark, he sees radiant light shining through the door he cannot enter.

Light shining through darkness when all is exhausted is an ancient theme. The Kafka story emphasises frustration, law and light beyond the power of man to embody, always just beyond reach. Yet, there is a hint of radiance. I am tempted to say the Light is our centre, as well as just beyond reach. For Kafka and Nachman, a distance element, tantalising or grim, is crucial (Kamenetz, 2010). Something holds the man fast, a promise of the law, a coming of light. For Nachman, devotion. For Kafka, I am not so sure, perhaps a yearning, a need, a refusal of anything less. Lack as illumination, uncompromising lack through which radiance glows.

Law and radiance, hidden radiance. I think of one of Andy Statman's CDs, *The Hidden Light*. Andy Statman is a clarinet and mandolin player and follower of Nachman. Much of his music gives expression to Jewish mysticism. Once a year, he plays his clarinet at Rabbi Nachman's grave in the Ukrainian town of Uman, where there is mutual infusion of spiritual power, grace, joy, devotion, sadness, and light.

But there is more to Kafka's story. The man does not have much longer to live after seeing the light. What strength he has left condenses into a question: everyone seeks the law. Am I the only one who tried to come in? Why is no one else here? The doorkeeper called the man insatiable, but answers, No one else is here because this is *your* door, yours alone, meant only for you. Now I must shut it. And the door closes as the man dies.

The doorkeeper called the dying man insatiable. It is not sex and aggression that is insatiable, but a burning for contact with Law and Light, a need to reach home base, a drive towards the Nourisher of All. The door closed forever is a real emotional nucleus in Kafka's life, the door meant solely for me, closed forever. A real state that Kafka explored in his stories: barred forever.

At some point, Kafka was taking Hebrew lessons and thinking of going to Israel, perhaps only a fantasy. But something stirred, turned on by *Ruach Elohim*, the Holy Spirit. A deep double state: faith deeper than faithlessness and faithlessness deeper than faith. A double reality.

Now a few more words about Nachman. As a child, Nachman spoke to God in heartfelt pleas. Some people stumble on God as children. Not the church or the temple—God. It just happens. People try to contain this happening with ritual and magical thinking. Moses contained his Vision, his Meeting, with Laws. Wherever there is a law, there is someone who cannot obey it. For example, Kafka's man who cannot go through the door cannot reach and live the law. Nachman spoke to God with his heart. Do you remember speaking to God with heartfelt pleas—with tears? I sure do, but histories and sensibilities differ.

Nachman developed speaking to God with his heart as a method, a kind of psychoanalytic method. He poured his heart out, all his faults, pains, misgivings, needs, and hopes. Outpouring that became a method, a method of prayer and inner growth. He differed from many religious authorities in that he advocated speaking your inmost feeling with any language that is natural to you. If the holy language, Hebrew, the official prayer language is not natural, speak in Yiddish, the prevalent tongue of his people. Speak in your native tongue, real and personal as you can. When I went through my most serious, orthodox phase, a rabbi I worked with, realising where I was coming from, said read the Bible in English. Pray in English. I grew into some Hebrew, some became part of me. But there is no need to pretend in front of God. He knows English is my mother tongue. There is nothing wrong with crying in English. Do not worry about the official prayers. Just make contact. For Nachman, heartfelt prayer was a path all life long.

More, he practised and taught his students not just a weeping heart, but a broken heart. To break your heart in speaking with God. I think of the prophets: turn your heart of stone to a heart of flesh. One reason I likened Nachman's "method" to psychoanalysis is because psychoanalysis is called a "talking cure". It is far more complex and subtle than this. But speaking is a big part of it. Saying whatever comes to you, feeling whatever comes, giving it voice. Nachman's broken-hearted speaking was like that. He was like Kafka in so far as he felt no matter how he poured his heart out, God did not notice him at all. He spoke, but was not heard. Over and over he had the experience of emotions not being met, perhaps like a baby whose cries are not heard, whose feelings meet oblivion. It seemed to him he was always pushed away as though he was unwanted.

The feeling he came up against often appears in dreams. In my experience, most people have dreams of being left out, unwanted, exclusion, exile, aloneness. Nachman maximised the feeling: utterly unwanted. Days and years pass and still he was far from Him, no sense of nearness at all. This state reminds me of the dying Jesus saying, "Father, why have you forsaken me?" What are Nachman and

Jesus finding? Not just destitution, but a most profound dimension of aloneness as part of the human heart.

The state Nachman undergoes requires sensitive thought. Nachman had a deep sense of intimacy with God, an unconscious, sometimes conscious or semi-conscious, nearness. Part of his sense of lack of nearness was that there could always be more nearness. His intimate nearness with God could not be exhausted. More was always possible. He could never be near enough. It is said that as the sage progresses, smaller and smaller "faults" seem bigger and bigger. In part, it might be something like this with Nachman: the sweetness of nearness made distance more painful. That there can always be more nearness magnifies distance. To be near is to be far. He would not be tormented by the nearness he did not have if he did not already taste nearness. He would not know to pray for a capacity that did not exist; more likely, he prayed for something he wanted more of. He could never have enough. I suspect his lack of closeness was more intimate than my greatest sense of nearness.

Nevertheless, we ought not minimise the state he expresses. Agonising distance from the Beloved, the Centre, the Place (*Hamakom*), becomes a path, a gate. Nachman did not budge. He refused to abandon his abandonment. He did not leave or escape for long the far from God moment. Reassurance did not help. He stayed with it and stayed with it year after year. I think of Bion speaking about certain emotional experiences as an unsolvable problem. What can you do with emotion as an unsolvable problem? Sit with it. Pay attention. Wait. If you sit with it without giving in to distracting "solutions", the problem might not change, but you will.

Nachman, at times, became depressed when, in spite of all his heart-rending pleas, no attention was paid to him and he remained far from God. Yet, if farness is what he felt, it became a link with the Most Intimate of All, the One who is closer to me than I am. Depression as link in response to loss of link. I am not suggesting you follow your depression to the bitter end, the very beginning, if that were possible. Nachman's path will not work for everyone. What I am suggesting, if less severe, still is challenging and freeing. Let in the state, in this case, distance, separation, loss, not having. It is a relief not to have to keep it away. One does not have to fight one's states or make believe they do not exist. To be able to let a feeling in and say, this is so, this is part of me, the way things are, the way I feel. A relief not to have to make believe it is not so. I do not have to fill the void with fillers just so it will be full.

At low points, Nachman would cease his private prayers for a number of days, then be overcome with shame for having called the goodness of God into question. What is this basic sense he has, the basic goodness that keeps on going down the tubes and recurring? He cannot get rid of basic goodness and he cannot hold on to it. He would begin again to plead as before. This sequence happened many times, a kind of basic rhythm. Not quite loss of faith–return of faith, but something like it. A decline of something important and refinding or reminding: loss of and refinding contact, dedication, renewal. Nachman remarked that he was in a constant state of renewal.

* * *

INTERMISSION

* * *

[There was a jump in the recording, so some of the seminar is lost.]
As a child, Nachman kept his dilemmas and problems hidden. It was as if he nursed himself a long time in a kind of psychic womb. In part, he felt his inner concerns would be damaged if they were aired. No one would understand. More, he felt what he was going through was beyond understanding. People would try to talk him out of it—it is not so bad, you will grow. He learnt at an early age that if you have deep intense states, people will try to get you out of them, minimise them, sweep them away. So, he kept them to himself. Psychoanalysis and esoteric traditions share concern with something hidden. Kabbalah purports to give the hidden, true, secret meaning of the Torah—the real meaning. And Freud purports to reveal what is hidden in the psyche. He calls the id the true psychic reality. Concern with secrets—something Kabbalah and psychoanalysis share.

It took Nachman a long time to come out and try to be the sage, the *tzadik* he felt he was. He would intermittently come out and then withdraw. In one state, he felt there was no revelation like his revelation. He felt he was the *tzadik hador*, the tzadik of the age. Other *tzadiks* paled by comparison, he was the one who really knew. In another state, he felt he knew nothing, was utterly unworthy. When he was younger, he shied away from controversy. He felt that controversy would damage you if you were not ready. On the other hand, he felt that if he revealed his teachings, people would faint. Who was ready to hear and bear the truths he knew? Like Kafka, he asked that his unpublished writings be burned after he died. Perhaps he feared they would be misunderstood and misused. No one was ready for the secrets, the revelations about the nature of our lives and our relationship with God. Something is trying to be born, but birth must not be rushed. Not an easy dilemma: to nurture the experiential, emotional work, the messengers, in secret, or enter public controversy and risk injury. A tension between gestation and delivery.

When Nachman revealed himself, he felt his teaching had no peer. He had an expansive aspect as well as a self-denigrating one. He saw other *tzadikim*, wise people, as finding their niche, their level. He, on the other hand, could not stay in a niche. Every moment he felt himself another person. Teachers entered into controversies from their niche. Since Nachman kept changing, reaching new levels, controversies that followed him could never end. In this state or attitude, Nachman wanted no hour to pass without further movement, constant struggle a path, necessary for growth, enabling him to move from place to place, opening heaven. Not only struggle with other teachers, but his own nature, sexual nature, for example. When students complained of exhaustion, he might reply that he would make peace if there were not spiritual places that could only be found through struggle.

Nachman noted that controversy was everywhere, between nations, within a family, individuals, groups. He felt all controversies were one, flowed from one source. In psychoanalytic terms, we might say they flow from us, from human nature, our makeup, our mix of love and aggression and much more. Sometimes the mix is more destructive, sometimes more generative. For Nachman to liken fights in the family to fights between groups outside the family shows keen psychological vision. He keeps his eye on fighting and its transformations. If we look at human history, fighting is one of the constants. Who fights whom changes, but fighting as an emotional link is an invariant. Wars continue although who fights whom over what shifts. It is the fact of war that Nachman puts a tracer on, whether in families or nations or oneself.

Even those who try to stay out of quarrels succumb. I think of patients who want peace. One meditates, another is lost is painting, deep immersion. They reach a place where it seems as if family frictions would be resolved. As one person said after an afternoon of peace, "I felt that now things would go better with my wife and kids." It took only a few minutes at the dinner table for all hell to break loose. We feel differently in different states, running the gamut of war and peace.

Nachman suggests that if war is in self, home, and nation, any place we can make a difference might affect other places. If we become less warring at home, will nations war less? I do not know about that. But at least home might become a little less of a war zone. Perhaps working with our emotional nature at any level can affect others. My hope is that every bit counts. But does it? It matters to *me*. Is that enough? Is there ever enough? If my life can be a little better, doesn't that count, too? What about the belief that if you affect anything at any level, you affect the whole cosmos?

One more remark on Nachman and war. He notes that if a man sitting alone in a forest goes mad, it could be because all the warring parties are now within. There are no others outside to divide the aggressive impulse with. Fighting with others saves us from going crazy, saves us from facing the aggression within. It is not just lack of contact that makes us go mad, but all the warring nations inside without any place to go. We are torn apart by ourselves. We can be grateful to our family, neighbours, nations for keeping us sane. We need someone to fight with.

On another note is the extravagance of Nachman's "highs". He felt that people would pass out if they heard his teachings. The world was not used to such high spiritual levels. The music of his teachings would evoke such longing and rapture that the whole of nature would sing in fulfilment beyond itself. All would faint in rapture as the soul of every being flew to height after height. This reminds me of a root meaning of ecstasy, to pass out of oneself, go beyond or outside oneself, "beside oneself". A sense of "crossing over" is part of many forms of spiritual experience. In Buddhism, there is "crossing over" of samsara to nirvanna (the "other side"). In the Bible, crossing over a river to another level of life is a recurrent image, from Abraham on, perhaps starting with Adam and Eve.

Nachman gives examples of everything singing. The land sings, the grass sings, each bit of existence with its own song. He talks about why some shepherds were musicians, like King David. The shepherd hears the earth singing and through his own song nourishes plants for his herds. Plants and flowers grow through song. The song of the shepherd includes the song of all beings and opens new possibilities. When asked how to answer an atheist, he answered, by song. Nachman had a magnificent sense of beauty and nature and song. There were periods when he felt that dancing would raise the souls of those who could not do it for themselves, and he would do nothing but dance. It was said that sometimes his dance was so still, so inward, you could not see him move. Stillness and movement were both important to him.

He travelled a lot, mirroring his restless soul, not content with what he achieved for long, sensing more. He uprooted his family depending upon need or intuition. One never knew where the spirit would lead. He was run out of one town for criticising the local *tzaddik*. Nachman claimed *he* was the *real tzaddik*, the *tzaddik* of the age, taking spiritual life to levels the local rabbi did not reach. He found his way to a town called Bratslav and became known as Nachman of Bratslav, where he established a school and had followers, before he went to Uman, where he is buried.

There were periods in Bratslav when clapping hands became important to him. Prayer should make you feel like clapping hands. If he did not hear clapping, he wondered if his students were really praying. Praying with one's whole being could take so many forms. Through a broken heart and a singing heart, through confession, struggle, dance, and clapping. The sound of one hand clapping? One universe clapping? All hearts breaking, singing, dancing, clapping.

When asked how to answer an atheist, he said, "Think about the depths of prayer, a moment your prayer was answered." In the depths of prayer, prayer itself is the "answer". It is not only a matter of prayers coming true, but of prayers being true. Certain moments of prayer open the deepest truths, often beyond words.

> A young man comes to his father, a rabbi and asks, "Rabbi, can you tell me how I can achieve what you have achieved?" How can he reach the spiritual place his father has? His father gives him texts to read. The son reads everything he was given and more, eager to search and grow. But he does not find what he is reaching for. Again he goes to his father and this time says, "Tata, I've read everything you gave me and I have not come close to finding what I am seeking."
>
> This time, the rabbi answers as a father, as tata. "When I read all this I did not find the Source of All Life either. Here is how it happened for me. When I was a young man, the Baal Shem Tov was speaking in

a town not far from mine, so I went to hear him. As I was walking, a blizzard came. My shoes were useless, my coat thin. I was afraid I would freeze to death. I was exhausted, I could not move. I cried and cried. Even in the blizzard I could not stop my tears. Before I knew it my tears became a prayer, "God, I can't move. I can't take another step. Please, please, help me hear the Baal Shem." At that moment, a horse and carriage came into view and brought me to the town. I followed lights in the windows to a little place that looked like a *shul* [house of worship and study]. The Baal Shem seemed to be waiting for me and said, "See? Your prayers are answered." The son understood. It was not from books but life, the prayer life is, that one lives the truth of one's being. (Paraphrased from Schachter-Salomi & Miles-Yepez, 2009, pp. 130–131)

The rabbi highlights a moment of desperation, prayer as outburst, outcry. It is not a luxury, frill, or decoration, but a lived moment of dread, loss, and love. Nachman generalises this moment as a path. He tells his students, speak from your heart in your own words, your own language. Speak in any way that breaks your heart. Speak your heart out to God. Words and tears from the depths of your life.

Nachman felt that descendents of the Baal Shem Tov had a special capacity to pour their hearts out to God because they were descendents of King David, whose psalms were such an outpouring. When I was being taught at Crown Heights in Brooklyn by the two old men I mentioned, they would say that the Messiah carries King David's soul and that there existed in our time someone who could carry that soul, their Rebbe Schneerson, but it was not happening. And though they were enjoined by their religion to expect the Messiah daily, they felt it was not likely to happen in their time, for whatever reason, but hoped it would in my time. Their sense of reality triumphed over wish-fulfilment, but the dream remained alive.

Let me summarise again three of the paths Nachman taught and lived: constant struggle; dance and song, music, beauty; and speaking from a broken heart.

Now, a few more notes to give a flavour of Nachman's life and teachings, with particular focus on emotional flavours. Feelings do have flavours, colours, sounds, and we have psychic taste buds.

There was a time when Nachman tried to attract students by going on retreat with them, living in the woods. The Baal Shem Tov loved being in the woods. Not only did he pray and meditate in the woods, but the woods itself was a kind of prayer. Nachman enticed some to come with him. He thought students might have a better chance of opening spiritual reality away from the routine they were used to. Parents of those who left home to follow Nachman did not appreciate this. Nachman tried many things to whet spiritual appetites.

One of his models was the biblical Abraham. A story is that Abraham went from town to town running through the streets, something like a madman in an alarmed, aggrieved state. This caused people to run after him to help him. Abraham used this as a ploy to talk about God. He was very persuasive to some and able to argue with many. Nachman, too, would do most anything to bring people close to God. Although such extraordinary means had their moments, they were not, on the whole, very successful. But Nachman's expressive attempts gradually strengthened his sense that he was the *tzadik* of the age, one who can see the needs of each soul, whose soul contained all souls and, by an intuitive sense, unlocked the souls of others.

A variation of the soul that contains all souls, is a sense that the *tzadik* contains what each soul lost by being born. Before conception and birth, each soul knows, and with birth "loses", awareness of what it is to do in life. Life partly is a search for what is lost at birth. The *tzadik* becomes a conduit, uniting souls with what they lost, so that they can come closer to fulfilling their missions. To do this, the *tzadik* must first find his own loss, a process that enables him to find the losses of others. An outcome is that the *tzadik* is a depository of everyone's losses. One finds one's own loss through the *tzadik*.

Here is another of the affinities between Nachman and psychoanalysis. We noted that Nachman's outpouring of the heart, saying all to God, has some resemblance to free association. There are ways of speaking whatever is in one that lead to growth. In Nachman's depiction of finding one's loss through the *tzadik*, we have a glimpse of Freud's emphasis on the analyst discovering within himself what he can help others find. We are aware, too, of how each person helps the other, journeys in mutual help.

[Question is asked that the tape did not pick up.]

There are lots of stories, myths, fables in Kabbalah. One that informs a thread that we are touching involves shattering of the vessels—Lurianic Kabbalah. Bion mentions Rabbi Luria, whom he describes as a carrier of the messiah–genius function. Bion contrasts what he calls

Establishment with Genius–Messiah aspects of personality, tensions between more conservative and more creative forces or tendencies in oneself, in groups, in society. Luria and Jesus are among those he cites as special carriers of the genius–messiah function, a creative function that breaks new ground in human vision and experiencing.

Luria was born in Jerusalem in the sixteenth century, studied in Egypt, and, through discussions with teachers from the distant past, including Elijah, he moved to Safed, Israel, where he mined his spiritual talents. Luria suggested that to make room for creation, God contracted. If God was everywhere and filled existence, how would there be room for the world and others? If God were merely expansive, would there be space for us? God's contraction creates a void making creation possible. Jacob Boehme, a German mystic, about fifty years later, also posited that God contracted to make room for creation. Luria, born in Israel, also had German roots. There were, across time and space, certain affinities between Luria and Boehme.

In a way, their logic, that God contracts to make room for creation, is lovely and fruitful as an image, but a curious curtailing of God. If God can do anything, God can fill all space *and* make space for existence (Chapter One, "Distinction–union structure" in *Contact With the Depths*, 2011). That God is everywhere *and* there is room for us is part of the mystery of creation. One need not posit a void for God to create. Yet void, or something like a void, is an important part of experience. And if God could do anything, God could contract, shrink, create a void. God *could* hold back to make room for us, although He did not have to.

To hold back and make room. By holding back, although He did not have to, God demonstrates an important moment: making room for others is an important capacity to develop. Often what we say about God pertains to aspects of our own makeup. If we were only expansive, we often would miss each other, we would not hear or see where the other was in a full sense. I often think of contraction as a kind of bow, making room for the other. Luria's spiritual imagination about God's relation to us opens possibilities about our relationship to each other and to our own self. For it is especially important that we also make room for ourselves.

Luria takes difficulties of creation to other levels, vision upon vision. Not only does God contract, but a contrary, expansive movement occurs within this contraction. An expansive movement that is meant to be contained, breaks through containment. God's emanations break some of the vessels meant to mediate the former. God could not contain His own energy. Some of the spheres mediating God's life (or power, force, energy, intention) broke. Higher spheres remained intact but lower spheres shattered under the impact. Higher and lower spheres or dimensions are depicted by the *Sephirotic* Tree, the Tree of Life, which charts flows of divine power through diverse centres, for example, will, wisdom, understanding, compassion, strength, beauty, down through the lower spheres having to do with action in our world (Appendix 1, "*Ein Sof* and the *Sephirot* Tree of Life"). The latter shattered under divine impact, with the implication that our world is, in a profound sense, shattered existence. The Shekinah, God's presence in our world, is depicted as feminine, yet torn. Our job is to help repair broken existence, heal earth's destiny, repair the broken vessels of God that transmit God yet create us. Some say our job is to help heal God and His Presence in the world, which involves healing ourselves.

The lower spheres are where we live, emotions in action. God is something like a two-year-old in a nursery, not knowing his own strength or impact. Things break. Dare one say that God is like a baby who does not know what he is doing? These images express feelings, our own relationship to the new. When we learn about something new we have to feel our way into relationship with it. In this vision, God is a beginner when it comes to creating our universe and us and has to learn what to do with the Powers he "uses", the Power he is. God is too much for his own energy. Perhaps he did not contract enough. Perhaps he cannot contract enough. Perhaps we are always in danger of uncontrolled outbreaks of godly energy. Creative energy was too much and spheres attempting to contain and mediate it broke. One of Bion's resonant themes is the importance of catastrophe in psychic life and difficulties involved in tolerating creative and emotional intensity of many kinds, a theme I hope to return to later.

Seminar member: The relationship between God and us is reciprocal. The breaking of the vessels teach us to make room for God. In the Japanese art of bonsai, the miniature plants, the plant is never planted in the middle of the container, it is always planted off-centre, because the centre is reserved for God. So, to learn that in one's own heart, there has to be something reciprocal, there has to be a nothingness to make room. I think the message of Luria is that if God could do this, then we can do this, too.

Response: That would be another ray in the circle (Appendix 3: "Circle and rays"), a positive ray. In the particular ray Luria delineates, brokenness, shatteredness becomes part of existence—pain, wretchedness, misery, suffering. One does not get around the fact of suffering. Yet, you are right to point out the importance of making room, working towards making room, which is part of learning, part of enlightenment. Luria adds to this a vision of buried sparks, divine sparks buried in brokenness and nothingness. Sparks that we can mine and help to release. Divine sparks buried in our own existence, our own psyche, our own lives.

An aspect of reciprocity is learning to become partners with our capacities. To let the work of enlightenment sparks release *us*. Divine sparks work in us, help in transformation. Buried sparks as creative potential, sparks of our own life, of divine potential. Winnicott, recall, speaks of a vital spark that is part of an infant's being, needing to be shepherded. Kabbalah teaches that we need to help release trapped sparks. Bear in mind, too, that these "sparks" work on us, in us, as stimuli of transformation. Bion writes of Transformations in O. We spoke about this earlier. A lot of transformational work goes on outside our awareness. The sparks themselves are busy helpers, part of the "material" of transformational processes. For example, in meditation, we often sense something going on, although we cannot say what. Something is happening, something in us is giving way, opening, changing, although we cannot pin it down. This is but one example of Transformations in O, work going on in psychic reality, elusive but making a difference.

Nachman, roughly two hundred years later than Luria, applied notions of higher–lower to teaching, how to talk to people. Kabbalah, like Aristotle and Plato, speaks of higher and lower functions, spiritual planes, levels of existence. Nachman was always trying to reach higher spiritual levels. In Nachman's terms, to be closer to God, one goes higher and higher, opening heavenly dimensions of soul. One could say this is a way of speaking, a way of giving expression to feeling, to inner facts or possibilities. God is not localisable up or down, right–left, here–there. God can be thought of as an inner point within, or no point anywhere. Judaism says no name or image will do. One could say there is a Greek influence in much up–down Kabbalistic thinking and vision. At the same time, up–down is a language related to our body, upright posture, head (eyes) over the rest. As a way to transcend or complement the upright and visual dominance, Bion repeatedly asks what life feels like through respiration, kinaesthesia, proprioception, skin, belly–mind, and Freud resorted to asking the patient to lie down and not face the analyst to gain some freedom from the upright. Many of you have thought of the association of hearing, listening, Sh'ma, hear, O Israel—listen. The Bible has passages suggesting be quiet, lie still, and hear God.

Higher and lower played an important role in spiritual direction, eliciting and heightening spiritual awareness. To people Nachman perceived to be on a lower, simpler rung, he would say, "God is everything everywhere." He would make it easy to find and boost faith. You cannot escape God. He is in everything you do. To those who were learned and secretly proud of their minds, he would say, "God is mysterious, unknown, ungraspable." A never-ending ancient lesson, God is not defined or confined by representations.

Nachman distinguishes between hidden and revealed faith. He was an observant Jew. He followed the Torah to the letter as best he could. As a mystic, there was a sense that Torah laws are conduits to God, paths of and to the One. On this level, there is a certain clarity, do's and don'ts, customs, rituals. A rabbi once explained to me that the laws and customs communicate what God wants of you. You do not ask a lover, why do you want it this way, not that way. You want to please the beloved; you do it. Yet, hidden dimensions beckon and attract Freud and Nachman, psychoanalysts and kabbalists. Often what is hidden is right before your eyes in plain view. In that case, the way one sees or fails to see is what makes something hidden or not.

Like Nachman, Wertheimer (Eigen, 2005; "Guilt" in *Emotional Storm*) says it is not a matter of reasons, but of life, experience. If you ask someone the reason for his faith, he might be able to give you a lot of good talk, but, at bottom, faith is its own reason. There is a point where reasons are not the point. Faith is. There are kinships throughout the Bible, passages speaking about God's faith, linking with Job's faith. Jesus: Father, why have you forsaken me? What kind of faith calls to God from the depths of forsakenness? What kind of faith is this when all has been taken away? What kind of faith when the One you call is gone, when there is no one to call? A faith for which you cannot give any reason. A bare heart's centre, nothing left. Nachman speaks of faith at the core of a broken heart, broken-hearted faith. "There is nothing so whole as a broken heart." One day he feels himself a man of clarity, a man of revealed religion. The next he is bare faith itself, broken, destitute, gratuitous faith—the thing itself. God gone, faith is the only link. God's presence is all the more acute in its absence. At such times, Nachman finds communication impossible, at other times, he speaks beautifully. There is something you cannot even tell yourself. You cannot tell yourself what it is, but it is. Would someone like Nachman be given medication today for states he felt were hidden messages from God? Would his world of experience be respected? Would some be nourished and enriched by it? Are we today enriched by it? Would we be the poorer had he not transmitted something of it?

[A seminar member asks a question relating faith to longing, faith as longing, not clear on the tape.]

Response: For Nachman, longing is part of a path. In certain moments, certain spheres or "rungs" of faith, it is a stimulant. You long for more, you long for further contact.

Seminar member: Or in the context of what you said before, longing for what you have but don't have ...

Response: Yes, exactly. Nachman said that everything has a heart, all of nature is alive with heart. The whole world has a heart, is heart. He depicts the world heart as an alive body, like the *Sephirot*, with head, hands, feet. His vision is great, magnanimous at such moments. He says that even the toenail of the world heart is more heart than any other heart. This reminds me of those moments when he feels he is living a day such as never was lived before, thinking a thought, praying a prayer such as never was thought or prayed before, from height to height, going beyond everything that ever was. Even the toenail of the heart of the world does this. This reminds me of Marion Milner (1987) writing about consciousness of the big toe.

Green (2004) writes of a Nachman story about a mountain spring at one end of the world, heart at the other. The heart longs for the spring and the spring longs for the heart. As one might expect, there are difficulties. The sun, eager for the heart and mountain spring to meet, shines so brightly that it burns the heart. This reminds me of how God, in creative exuberance, shattered some of the vesssels (*sephirot*) of creation. The sun, like God, eager to help, forgets its own strength. Such tales mirror our fragility in relation to our own energies.

The sun burns the heart while the heart cries in longing for the spring. We are caught between too much and too little, too much aliveness, too much deadness, burnt by our desire for more aliveness. Yet, the heart keeps going. When it must rest, a great bird spreads its wings over it, protecting it. This reminds me of Faust falling asleep when he discovers that Beatrice killed herself, the healing work of deep sleep. Or the fig tree God caused to grow to give shade to Jonah, hovering over all the complexities of a complicated heart.

If the heart is filled with so great a desire for the spring, why doesn't it simply enter the spring? There are complications. One is that the mountaintop keeps disappearing, or almost disappearing. In a mystical way, the spring is the life of the heart. If the mountaintop where the spring flows should vanish, the heart would die. Back and forth: it cannot have the spring, it cannot be without the spring. The spring flows through the heart but no one knows how. If the former was lost to heart vision, not only would the latter die, the whole world would be destroyed. Existence depends on a delicate link between spring and heart.

This brings us to a fourth path. We have constant struggle, dancing and singing, and speaking from a broken heart. The fourth root of faith involves awareness that one has no understanding at all. Ignorance, not knowing as a path. It is paradoxical how deep one can go, and how fully one can open by going through the gate of not understanding. Nachman straddled worlds. One day he "knew". One day he didn't. Knowing is good, he said, but my I don't know is better. Faith based on revealed truth is good, but deeper faith has no proof or reason. Nothing to hold on to but faith itself, "faithfulness in the night". Akin to Job's faith, everything stripped away, or Jesus' cry from forsakenness. Calling from the depths, the night.

If I love God with all my heart and soul and might, with everything in me, in so far as this is possible, my hate loves God. If I love God with all I am, then my hate loves God, I love God with my hate as well. We know from Freud how affects, pronouns, and states reverse. Reciprocity and reversal between hate and love, between doubt and faith. My doubt loves God. My unbelief loves God. My atheism loves God. Can I say my faith hates God? There are ways that this is so. We have this fluidity.

Nachman speaks of the wholeness of faith. He affirms the questioning mind, the technical and scientific mind, without which we would not have a building to be in or a sound system to speak through. We would not have the books that form a basis of our study in our meeting today. Yet, Nachman expresses a tension between the mind that asks for reasons and a faith no "reason" can encompass. A little like Winnicott saying you ought not ask a child if he created or discovered the breast or prepossessing object of interest. The child should not have to make such a decision when immersed in a significant experience. If the child is immersed in illusion, it might, for a moment, be paradoxical, creative illusion, nourishing being.

A variant of Nachman's vision of wholeness involves wholeness of the universe, in which anything can become anything else. He speaks of the universe as a *dreidel*, a spinning top, in which life forms turn into each other. One might almost be reading passages from Chuang Tzu (1964). A head may turn into a foot and vice versa. Angels and men transform into each other. High becomes low, low high. All manner of separations and blends of spiritual and material qualities occur. He stresses a common root. For a resonant depiction, see Bion's diagrams of a single root at the origin of various phenomena and categories. (*Cogitations*, 1994b, p. 323; Appendix 4, O-grams.) In this vision, Nachman and Bion overlap in depicting transformational processes emanating from a common source.

Nachman's vision of everything transforming into everything else, and Nachman's and Bion's sense of common origin (O) or root, is a basis for compassion. Bion writes of different ways of using or relating to truth, depending on attitude, disposition, sense of life: cruel or compassionate use of truth. Nachman spoke of love as a basis for life before there was Torah. The biblical patriarchs lived through love, God's love, before God gave Moses the Torah. Inherent love was the guide. One could argue Torah always existed, or that there is no temporal before–after when it comes to God. Torah is eternity, part of eternity, infinite. But in our time-world, in the depiction of before–after, love came first.

Similar questions can be raised with regard to God's withdrawal to create the world. Everything is God, filled with God: how can there be nothing, "space" void of God? Nachman leaves such questions unanswered. From his point of view, all will be clear in heaven. But in terms of methodology on earth, he places importance on not knowing. Not knowing becomes a spiritual and psychic path, shedding, deepening, quickening, opening.

There might be other ways of experiencing, akin to Freud's primary process or Matte-Blanco's symmetrical mode of being (Eigen, 2011, "Distinction–union structure" in *Contact With the Depths*.) A dimension might exist in which God is and is not everything. If God can do anything, God can do that. Bion wrote that for a thing to be, it is and is not at the same time. Aspects of psychoanalysis tap experiential possibilities often overlooked, dimensions in which the law of contradiction does and does not hold. Openness to different experiential possibilities feed each other.

I would like to read something from Chuang Tzu (1964) that is hard to pass up, about everything turning into everything else.

> Joy, anger, grief, delight, worry, regret, fickleness, inflexibility, modesty, willfulness, candor, indolence – music from empty holes, mushrooms springing up in dampness, day and night replacing each other before us, and no one knows where they sprout from. Let it be! Let it be! It is enough that morning and evening we have them, and they are the means by which we live. Without them we would not exist, without us they would have nothing to take hold of . . . I do not know what makes them the way they are. It would seem as though they have some true Master, and yet I find no trace of him. He can act – that is certain. Yet I cannot see his form. Whether I succeed in discovering his identity or not, it neither adds nor detracts from his Truth. (pp. 32–33)

Here is another another passage:

> All at once Master Yu fell ill. Master Ssu went to ask how he was. "Amazing!" said Master Yu. "The Creator is making me all crookedy like this! My back sticks up like a hunchback and my vital organs are on top of me. My chin is hidden in my navel, my shoulders are up above my head, and my pigtail points at the sky. It must be some dislocation of the yin and yang! . . . My, my! So the Creator is making me all crookedy like this! (pp. 80–81)

Master Yu goes on reflecting that perhaps the hidden one will turn his arm into a rooster to announce the day, or a bow to shoot prey for food. Each transformation has uses. There are so many changes, it is best to be free of being bound by them.

You might be astonished to find a radical reincarnation view in Nachman and its fit with ancient imagery, as well as the theme of not knowing. For Chuang Tzu and Nachman: we really do not know (Eigen, 2011, "I don't know" in *Contact With the Depths*). Along this line, when Buddha was asked metaphysical questions, he might say something like, "Just keep meditating. Those are questions I cannot answer. Keep practising."

Questioner: . . . I have faith, and I can't explain it, and I can't say I have faith . . .

Response: There are all kinds of faiths and paths and possibilities. Everyone speaks her and his reality. There are happier versions of faith, perhaps, than the faith I am touching, which often (not always) has a tragic element. There is an urge to talk people out of dark places, but for some, that is a greater horror than living in the dark. There are terrible truths vital for living. To lose them can be losing a chance to be born. You tell a child, "It was only a dream, a nightmare", implying it is not really real, things will look different in daylight. But there comes a time when nightmares are vital to one's growth, expressions of psychic realities, traumas, binds, difficulties. When I saw Bion and told him some troubling dreams, he sided with the dream figures, saying, "Your dream is real. The feelings and images are real." Emotionally real, real feeling.

What I am trying to convey today, in part, is expressed by the circle and ray diagram (Appendix 3): common nucleus, many radii. A simple diagram, too simple, it signals common roots and many offshoots. Perhaps we have many nuclei and radii, cores and offshoots. Even shared originating processes take different forms. So many paths and possibilities. Are we recognisable to each other? To ourselves? If we are unrecognisable, can we learn to respect that state of affairs? Something in us needs and wants to respect complexity. But perhaps something cannot bear it.

[Inaudible question.]

Response: There can be faith–love, there can be faith–truth, there can be bad faith, but the latter is not the faith we are talking about. We are talking about faith as such, which nothing can kill. For example, facing the worst that can be faced, yet faith resurfaces. How is that possible? For many, it happens.

Questioner: The withdrawal, the shattering, I have trouble with the concept that it was wrong. What I am trying to say is, there is no wrong in God. I accept the shattering and I accept the withdrawal as necessary for there to be room for human life. Shattering, withdrawal are parts of the model for our lives.

Response: I accept your acceptance, but do you accept my experience? I talked about something going wrong in creation, the breaking of vessels, the shatter. A sense that runs through history of something wrong, something off. Shakespeare and Blake write of a "worm" in human experience, a canker in the rose. What is this sense of something wrong? You might be saying this sense of something wrong is itself wrong? A misconception, illusion? Yet, I wonder about the danger of dismissing it prematurely, when it seeks to make contact, needs attention. I find myself a little in the position of a child who is told his nightmare is not real.

Questioner: Oh, it's experience. Oh, OK, I accept your ray. I accept all your rays.

Response: Thank you.

Questioner: I've been pondering since you said "my hate loves God", which is a little different, I think, than the dreidel. We are not talking about hate transforming, we are talking about love coming out of an experiential state that is still named and still identifiable as hate. Could you say something about that?

Response: I think you are doing a good job right now of explicating what you want to explicate. Do you want to say more about it?

Questioner: It has just got me very excited. Hate still exists, it is still identifiable, but love can come out of something. It is not transformed.

Response: Freud is so rich, you can put many things in so many parts of the text. Reading Freud is endless. One of the things in Freud: nothing is lost. Nothing is lost, whatever transformations you go through. Don't expect landing in Israel to make it all go away. *You* are still there.

Questioner: Well if the hate is not there, I don't know . . .

Response: Well, if the hate is still there, you are not?

Questioner: If the hate is not there, then you are not.

Response: No danger. Yes?

Another questioner: I'd like to say something about what I've been experiencing, which is that I feel your words have become my nervous system, like strands of a lyre, and you are strumming me, and what is coming out is everything I know getting in the way of everything I don't know. But alongside of being filled up with my own knowledge, which is resonating with everything that you say, is also a feeling of immense love for you. And in that love, which I've had for a very long time, I'm feeling tremulous. And in that tremulousness, I have the faith that I can carry away what I can contact in this room and reach what I don't know. And if I do, I will then bring you the question that I cannot form now, because all that I know is getting in the way.

Response: I love you and I have no answers to anything but I do try to respond. Sometimes, as with some of the questions today, my responses are not too good. But don't give up on me.

Questioner: What I love, what I feel, is your goodness. You are good for me. You have always been good for me.

Response: From your mouth to God's ear. When the day comes, I'm going to say, "Well, one person said I was good for them!" So it better be real, because nothing else is going to get me out of that jam.

Questioner: It is real because I saw you for two sessions in 1972, and that made a permanent alteration in my life.

Response: Thank you.

Questioner: What you said when I left—I brought you a conflict—what you said was, "That's a good conflict to have," which completely opened the door for me, and I knew it was a door I had to walk through, which is a life of constant struggle.

Response: Yes, it's true. I guess I am saying that in some ways today, too.

Questioner: Tales from the dark side. I was wondering if faith might be linked to wisdom related to a kind of loss or sacrifice; the willing release of memory, knowing and desire is a kind of death. Also the darkness you speak of—a kind of death, a way of dying.

Response: That is beautifully put. We have polarities, no? Plenitude and emptiness, loss and fullness. All the parts of our beings are the colour of our life. Kafka called life an incomplete moment. If life is an incomplete moment, certainly this one is also. This might not be true for all people at every moment. I can verify what you are saying by a different example. To get along with someone, you have to tolerate loss or there will not be room for how the other sees you. You have to make room for the other. If you only want the other to see you according to your desires, you want your desire to capture the other's desire (or vice versa). You can have some good times that way, but sooner or later it is going to hurt. Something is going to happen to break that fusion, illusion, megalomania. If you cannot build up tolerance for loss, for example, loss of how the other sees you, loss of how you want to see the other, loss involving unfulfilled desires and images, if you cannot tolerate loss, you cannot tolerate a relationship. On the other hand, if you can tolerate such loss, there is much to gain.

[Question about taking a rest from the law, although the tape is partly inaudible.]

Response: I think we need a lot of downtime from law. Law can be too much for us. You have to take it with a grain of salt, a little flexibility. When I went through a pretty radical orthodox phase—strictly observing *Shabbos* (Sabbath), being kosher, whatever else I could do—my family suffered terribly. I hear from many orthodox people that getting through *Shabbos* can involve a lot of wear and tear. The idea of rest can be idealised when you are dealing with wretched kids. I knew one dedicated man who got through *Shabbos* by sleeping much of the day. Reality is one thing, ideal another. Yet, there are many for whom strict observance is beautiful or has beautiful aspects.

Nachman was observant. For him, like many Jewish mystics, the laws are ways to get closer to God, avenues of contact. We can follow him and go into the woods together and reach great heights. But, in reality, we come back to our affectional ties, daily existence, city life. Whether you are observant or not, whatever path you follow or discover, we come to something mysterious. We participate in a sense of mystery. It is a root moment that connects our lives. Taoism says, "Stay with the situation as it is. If you impose right and wrong, true and false, you will likely make a bigger mess". Hard enough to stay with things as best you can without trying to treat them as you think they ought to be.

You talked about taking a rest from the law. I was thinking that maybe that is what God does on *Shabbos* when He rests. Law can be too much for God, too. As babies, as children, we spent a lot of moments without the Law. Immersed in play, in fascination, timeless. I think, too, of Nachman saying that we lived by love before the Law. The Law gives us *Shabbos*, which is beautiful, then makes *Shabbos* unhappy, so many details to watch out for. For some, all the observances are second nature. Even so, there can be unwanted consequences. For a time we had Friday night dinners with an ecstatic rabbi, who fell asleep at the table. He could not keep his head up or eyes open out of fatigue. His *Shabbos* chores and preparation were too much for his constitution. His wife looked at him apprehensively, knowingly, tending to the table and the children.

A phrase, "We lived a long time without it", comes back to me. I heard Anna Freud say it at a meeting in London in 1975. André Green spoke about changes in psychoanalysis, using Winnicott, Bion, Lacan, Freud. He outlined basic dynamics of borderline psychosis. As I listened, I felt psychoanalytic imagination was alive. Leo Rangell spoke about the structural theory as it was used in the USA. He spoke a lot about superego. I felt deadened. The two talks seemed to represent diverse spirits and interests. I heard of further complications behind the scenes. Rangell was in the Los Angeles Psychoanalytic Society. When Bion migrated to Los Angeles in the last decade of his life, the Los Angeles Society denied this creative man (and former president of the British Society) full status. Perhaps he did not fit their picture of psychoanalysis. Creativity and difference is often defended against. Near the end of the meeting, Anna Freud, in old age, got up and said, "Structural theory, structural theory. We lived a long time without it." An unexpected moment, a breath of air, an affirmation of creative spirit. A thirty-nine-year-old man at the meeting, me, felt she responded to the same enlivening and deadening spirits that I did.

You might say Rangell's use of the structural theory was a kind of deadening use of the law, while Green explored ins and outs of processes that opened doors of madness. So, yes, the law has its functions, but you have to watch out. Everything is dangerous. The law is dangerous. No law is dangerous. As Bion would say, there is no substitute for your own intuition, your own sensing, feeling, your faith sense. Try to do justice to your experience. And, like a baby, who cannot take too much consciousness, take time off as needed or as circumstances allow.

Question: Doesn't rage grow out of desire?

Response: It can, and desire can be more than sexual. Nachman got overly stuck on eradicating sexual desire but, if you want to put it that way, there are scarier desires, like subjugation. Slavery was part of human life for quite a long time and, one way or another, even if only inwardly, still is.

Rage can be complicated. If it is linked with desire it can be a need to always be right. Or a need to feel omnipotent, or strong, or powerful. Or an inability to face a sense of helplessness and work with it ("impotent rage"). Rage can be one of the most orgasmic, total states. It short-circuits complex psychic functioning. It blots out (a biblical phrase) complex awareness. It might be a response to sensed injustice and injury. Whether or not it has a positive function depends on many factors. In my book, *Rage* (2002), I comment that a sense of being right has done more harm in human history than most other attitudes. Rage feeds on a sense of being right.

Question: Life is such a mixture and you have written about the mixtures of feelings compellingly. You have included a sense of the holy. Can you say something about this now?

Response: Here is a story I think I told you in our first seminar. A lot of new people are here today, so I will risk repeating it. Maybe something a little different will happen this time around. When I was a child, an old man would come to our house once or twice a year for a donation. His name was Rabbi Kellner. My father would stop whatever he was doing and greet him and respond to his requests. When Rabbi Kellner came, he brought a light with him, a glow. Mostly centred around his face, his head. His forehead, cheeks, beard, eyes—a glow that varied in shades, bright white light to golden. When he talked to me I lit up.

I felt something like it when my clarinet teacher played for me at the end of lessons. The sounds tickled me and I could not stop laughing. He would threaten to stop playing if I did not stop laughing, but I could not help myself.

The glow I experienced with Rabbi Kellner I later came to recognise as a sense of the holy. I suspect the laughter I felt with my clarinet teacher was a soul reflex to being tickled by beauty. The soul can be tickled by beauty and glow with the holy. Through Rabbi Kellner, I experienced the holy as embodied and real.

During the time I said Kaddish for my father, a rabbi referred me to Rabbi Kastel in Crown Heights, Brooklyn, and when Kastel heard my story he suggested I study with two old men in Crown Heights—Rabbi Kellner's sons! This was over fifty years after my childhood meetings with their father! Here I was, a fifty-year-old man, studying with the aged sons of a rabbi who mediated a holy glow in my childhood.

They told me many things. One that comes back to me now because we were speaking about rage—when the Messiah comes there will be peace on earth. If a man lifts his hand to strike another an angel will stop it. (I recently found online an article I wrote for *The Jewish Review* in 1987, soon after my father died, about experiences that brought me closer to the mysterious sense we hover with: http://thejewishreview.org/articles/?id=66.)

As for the mixtures you mention: we have emotional capacity capable of experiences that seem to go beyond what we call real. But they are very real and help shape our existence. In emotional reality there can be maximum destructiveness and maximum love. How is this possible? A sense of the Good, Beauty, Holy, Justice intertwined, opposed to, fused with destruction. That we recoil at this notion indicates that we are afraid to let in fully our experiential capacity. We shut off experience to let in what we can manage. At the same time, we sense there is more that we simply are not up to. To reach a point where we will not have to strike each other to defend our smaller emotional territories, we need to acknowledge the more we cannot access. To live in this More, in awareness of this More, to make a sense of the More a living part of us, an essential part, might help to take the edge off our need to affirm and defend little portions of "self" at others'—and our own—expense.

Time is almost up and there is so much to say and do. We have touched several of the threads that Kabbalah has in common with psychoanalysis, but far from the seventeen I counted before the seminar started. For the remaining moments, I would like to say a few words about Bion. I am looking at *Cogitations* (1994b, pp. 234–235).

Among the threads we have waded into is the thread of not knowing, unknowing, realisation, and confession that one does not know, faith without knowing (Eigen, 2011, Chapter Three, "I don't know"). It appears in many ways in many places in Bion. One extraordinary passage is on pp. 234–235.

For Bion, what is the core of a dream? Emotional experience is the core of a dream. Emotional experience, for good or ill, is not only the core of a dream, but of the psyche. In the passage we are looking at he distinguishes

> between the experience that consists in trying to understand an emotional experience that is secondary to the attempt to solve a problem, and the experience that consists in trying to solve a problem in which the emotional experience itself is the problem. (p. 234)

For the former, we have the arsenal of induction, deduction, analytic and logical thinking, common sense, hypothesis, inference, various cognitive operations involved in problem solving, including the "feel" of a situation, "hunches", goal directed intuition, selected facts that jell *gestalts*, various mental syntheses. We seek solutions, synthesising material we gather together. This is an important use of mind, spanning means–end relations, goals, purpose, learning how things work and how we see things, issues of creative construction and regulation.

Bion writes, in the second instance in which emotional experience itself is primary and problematic, "there is probably no way of regarding the problem as anything at all" (pp. 234–235). This is one of Bion's most dramatic ways of pointing to radical unknowing when it comes to our most basic emotional life. It is a situation we try to extricate ourselves from as soon as possible, seeking psychic organisations that seem to offer meaning and coherence. That is, we have little tolerance for the radically unknown nature of emotional life, finding ways out of this situation by turning it into something we imagine can be worked with by usual means (e.g., operations like those noted above).

Bion continues, "In short, there are situations that are felt to be problems that either have no solution, or to which no solution can be found with the equipment at the disposal of the individual experiencing them" (p. 235).

I should let Bion's statement sit as a psychoanalytic *koan*. Please come back to it in its raw nakedness. It is a statement that undresses the psyche and reveals it in its nudity. But I will spend a little time meandering around it.

The various mental operations I listed are among those that might be circumscribed by Bion's notion, K, knowing, knowledge, the pursuit of knowledge. The domain he touches by directing attention to the situation in which emotional experience is itself a primary problem opens a "dimension" he calls F, faith. He describes faith as the psychoanalytic attitude, a state of being without memory, expectation, understanding, or desire (a discipline or process or gesture towards such a "state"). He quotes a letter in which Keats wrote of a capacity to be "in uncertainties, Mysteries and doubts, without any irritable reaching after fact and reason". In *Attention and Interpretation* (1970), he notes that F discipline can open a state of "hallucinosis", a counterpart to psychotic hallucination, making it possible to link with psychotic individuals from the inside, "psychosis to psychosis".

He is not saying K is bad and F is good. Capacities change values depending on how they function in given contexts. Either, so to speak, can be good or bad, or good and bad. Bion supports exploring capacities and seeing where they lead, unending explorations with unending mysteries (when it comes to F) and problems (when it comes to K). His method, partly, is a kind of psychic seeing and sensing, psychic vision and bracketing of vision, F-intuition. Freud spoke of consciousness as a kind of psychic sense organ. For Bion, F is a kind of psychic organ or attitude or path that opens walls to infinity.

K is more akin to Buber's I–It relation, akin to engineering, regulation, means–end relations, manipulation of experience. F is non-manipulative, seeking contact with the thing itself, akin to Buber's I–Thou (1970). Part of growth towards F involves struggle to be less manipulative, more open to experience. Even with little success, such struggle can be beneficial. There is no one universal prescription for growth in the F-dimension, F-growth.

When emotion itself is the problem, how do you tolerate emotion? Freud wrote about how frustrating tolerating the build up of states can be. Dewey (2005) in *Art As Experience,* wrote beautiful passages about difficulties in tolerating the build-up of intensity in experiencing a work of art. He offered hints in training oneself to enable experiencing to build. We tend to short-circuit experience. I remember

Alan Ginsberg's description of going to the Museum of Modern Art, high on marijuana, the latter enabling him to stand still and stare at a painting for a long time and begin to *see* it.

To tolerate a feeling without quite knowing what it is, sensing its rise and fall, shifts of quality and intensity, no name or image or conception as yet, just the feeling itself. A little like getting used to seeing in the dark. One might begin to see or imagine or sense related networks, veins, branches, links with other quasi-mute perturbations. One could pursue these in K modes of relating, often with profit. But we come back to F again, F in O, T in O, facing unknown reality, intangible, ineffable infinities and transformational events.

Freud and Klein, in various ways, point out difficulties in staying with emotional life. We cannot stay with feelings for long. We shunt, displace, symbolise, evacuate, substitute, reverse, turn emotional sensations or inklings or premonitions into something else. It is very hard to stay with experiencing as such. To see a feeling through, to live it through, especially if it is nameless, shapeless, homeless, is a task awaiting development. To pay attention to this difficulty might stimulate development. One can begin to appreciate in a new light Nachman's sense that emotions are God's messengers, expressive vehicles of unknown processes. Bion highlights difficulties of staying with unknown feelings in unknown ways, yet affirms the importance of trying to do so. In F, there is nothing to hold on to, yet one may sense intimations of an unknowing "sensing" process, a "faithing" process.

Bion emphasises the need to build capacity to stay with experience, in so far as that is humanly possible. The capacity to work with emotion as a problem is embryonic, perhaps scarcely conceived. To grow the capacity to work with, support, tolerate, digest emotional life is an evolutionary challenge. Bion calls attention to this problem, notes it. We are not going to do justice to it. We are not going to draw up a plan of attack. At this point, we would not know what we were trying to approach. Bion cultivates awareness that how to approach emotional experience *is* a problem. We wait on a capacity that has not yet arrived, or is gestating, perhaps in process of slowly being born.

Levinas (1999) speaks of a new attitude, "maturity for insoluble problems", requiring waiting on emotional or attitudinal difficulties for which no solution is apparent. Need for growth connected with affective attitudes exerts pressure that lacks words, thought, definition, a state that in some way "may resemble sleep". Levinas calls upon a passage from St Exupery in which the little prince asks the pilot to draw a sheep. The pilot fails to draw one that the little prince accepts, then draws a parallelogram, a box in which a sheep sleeps, to the little prince's pleasure. Then Levinas concludes:

> I do not know how to draw the solution to insoluble problems. It is still sleeping in the bottom of the box; but a box over which persons who have drawn close to each other keep watch. I have no idea other than the idea of the idea of the idea that one should have. The abstract drawing of the parallelogram—cradle of our hopes. I have the idea of a possibility in which the impossible may be sleeping. (1999, p. 89)

To wait on a capacity not yet born or conceived, or one that is gestating, or slowly being born. Bion writes of ways we prematurely extricate ourselves from this situation. Sometimes, I think of what it would be like if the whole world, every single person, top to bottom, chanted in synchrony three words little used in high places: "I don't know". A world-wide wave of unknowing together. It takes so much effort to pretend to know and to act as if one were better than one is, more whole and knowing, and the cost to individuals and nations is high.

An emotional problem without a "solution" or equipment to work with it exerts pressure on personality. We can try to escape the pressure or try to stay with it, to the extent we can. In either case, pressure builds. If we stay with the problem without solution and the equipment to meet it does not arrive, the problem makes demands on us, on our ability and capacities. It makes demands on personality and thought. One thing that can happen when you stay with an emotional experience with no solution—Nachman's "constant struggle" in an intermittent way—you keep coming back to it: *it* may not get "solved" but *you* change, *you* grow in the process. The problem might or might not give way, but something happens to you. Batting your psyche against an unsolvable problem forces you to develop. In my chapter, "I killed Socrates" *in Flames From the Unconscious* (2009), I wrote of a psychic "wormhole". The intensity of pouring oneself into an insoluble problem perforates the psyche and you find yourself in another place, a place you might not have imagined before it happened. The unsolvable can promote growth of experience in unsuspected ways. Well, I guess we will have to leave it at that for now, our time has run out. The seminar as an incomplete moment, a sense of beginning.

APPENDIX 1

Ein Sof and the *Sephirot* (Tree of Life)

*E**in Sof* is a notation for the unnameable, inconceivable, unimaginable, unrepresentable—what in English we call "God". The words mean without boundaries, boundless, no bounds, represented as infinity or infinite infinite. In a way, it is beyond God, as the latter is a notation with a wide range of associations and meanings that limit its unknowability (the use of "it" is already a misappropriation). I personally sometimes think of Sofia, wisdom, already a vast limitation. With the popularity of Buddhism, one might speak of *Ein Sof* as no-thing and its twin emanation, being.

Technically, *Ein Sof* is not part of the *Sephirot*/Tree of Life. It is beyond all representation. You might envision it as the Energy that flows through the *Sephirot* and "creates" them. Unrepresentable Primal Power, or Presence. Again, these are terms drawn from our phenomenology of force, action, experience, care, and mystery. I should say at the outset that everything I say is hypothetical, fantasy, attempts to express the inexpressible, touch the intangible that touches me. Bion speaks of O, unknown, unknowable ultimate reality, not identical with *Ein Sof*, but not unrelated.

There are ten *Sephirot* and an additional hidden one (*Daat*). The divine flow goes through *Keter*/crown, roughly the head *chakra*. It

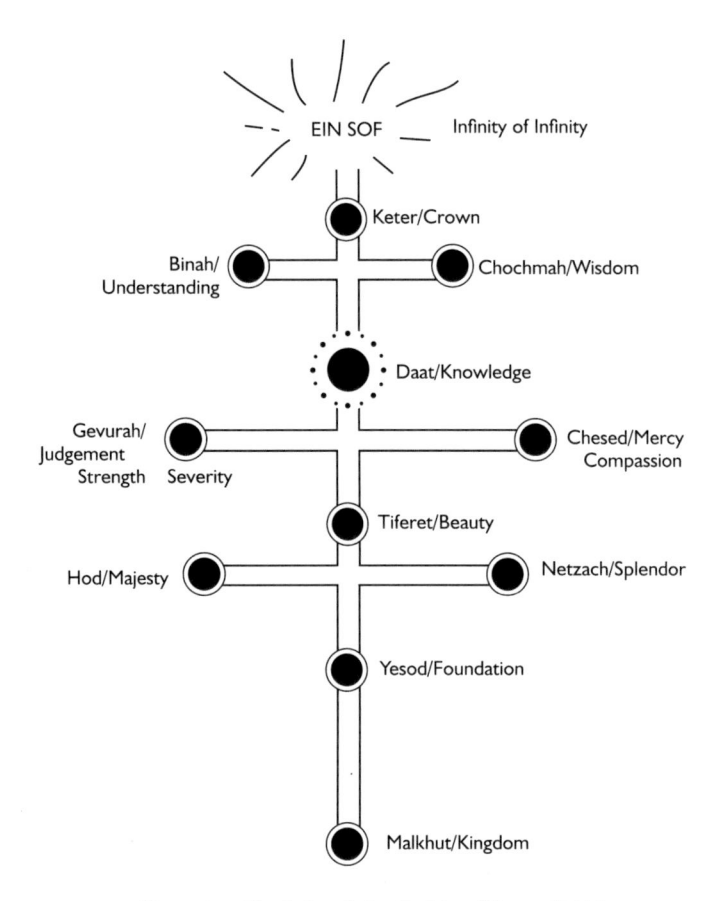

Figure 1. Ein Sof and the *Sephirot* (Tree of Life).

could be described as intention, will, or humility. *Keter* is an emanation of *Ein Sof*. If it is divine will or intention (very restrictive terms) it means a willing to life, to create life and open dramas of existence, a generative stream through all levels of possibility. As the drama unfolds, death is part of the stream.

From *Keter* the flow passes through *Chochmah*/wisdom, often depicted as a divine flash akin to "insight"—a sudden blast of white light containing all colours. Mozart described such relative moments when a symphony appeared to him in an instant, and all he had to do was work it out. Saint Paul describes something like this when, in a flash, he was thrown by divine impact and all at once knew Christ. It remained for him to elaborate and develop his revelation and relationship to divinity and the Divine Presence. I call these happenings "relative" because they appear to be relative levels of what is meant by *Chochmah*, immediate, wordless, imageless impact and response. The narrative, or musical or visual forms that emerge to express felt impact, the instant "blast", is relative to one's moment in history, the way one uses language, the nature of one's understanding. The "thing itself" eludes all "formulations" that sensed reality gives rise to. My use of "instantaneous impact" is also qualified. In actual living, *Chochmah*, wisdom, might grow slowly over a lifetime, a cumulative fruition through many experiences. In this case, rather than hitting all at once or in spurts, it sneaks up on one over time. For simplification of communication here, I will use my wording of impact and response.

We are impelled, called upon to work with wordless, imageless impacts, mine them as best we can. From *Chochmah* the flow passes through *Binah*/understanding. The divine impact works on us and we have to work to understand. We think of God's understanding as true, ours as relative, subject to error, bias, limitations, yet necessary. We cannot evade the task of understanding, for, whatever we do, however we live, we understand things one or another way. Our understanding, our "take" on life, impacts on how we live or fail to. This is one reason Socrates spoke for the importance of examining understanding: we often think we know things that we do not, sometimes with injurious consequences. What we understand and the way or how we understand affects the quality of our existence.

From *Binah*/understanding, the divine flow goes through *Daat*/knowledge, the hidden sphere on the tree. It is said to be directly connected to *Ein Sof* as well as a way station in the circuits of capacities. In its direct connection, it is Godly knowledge, knowing God. As a conductor or sphere in the divine flow, it forms a kind of triangle: *Chochmah, Binah, Daat*: Wisdom, Understanding, Knowledge. With *Keter*, a quaternity, or inverted triangle. The light of wisdom transmits through understanding, which transmits knowledge, all transmitting Divine Life–Intention (*Keter*) flowing from *Ein Sof*. We might write this with double arrows: *Ein Sof*, no-thing, infinite of infinites ↔ fullness of being, indicating reciprocal links between capacities. Some mystics emphasise the downward flow (Chabad) and some the flow from below upwards (Nachman), but these are points of emphasis, for the flow cannot be circumscribed by directions (God exceeds directions).

The *Sephirot* have multiple references and act as kind of mirror images between Godly capacities and human capacities. The *Sephirot* function both as God's medium for creation and as human capacities to realise divine life. Our capacities can be used for many purposes. Human wisdom, understanding, knowledge can make atom bombs, medicine, beautiful buildings, wondrous art, enlightenment journeys. There seems no end to what we can do with our capacities, good and ill. At the same time, the work of capacities can open us to the Unknown more deeply, fully, growing contact with the Deepest of All. Some express this by trying to lead a godly life in a human way. But one cannot trap or exhaust *Ein Sof* with mind or story or intention. Yet, a point of contact keeps speaking to us, through us. Touched by the Untouchable.

Through *Daat*, the divine flow passes from *Keter–Chochmah–Binah* (wisdom–understanding–knowledge) to *Chesed*/mercy, loving compassion, the right hand of God. Then from *Chesed*/mercy to *Gevurah*, judgement, the left hand of God. In human terms, the dialectical mixture of both love and judgement are needed. The dangers of one without the other is harshness and severity on the one hand, mush on the other. Each contributes to the balance and growth of the whole. I think of Jesus telling his disciples, "Be harmless as doves, prudent as serpents." A wedding of care and discernment. The Hebrews in the Bible often were called stiff-necked, stubborn. They would not have survived otherwise. Neither would they have survived without a most profound love and knowledge of God in their hearts and souls, however great their stubborn resistance to the commandments.

From *Gevurah* the flow passes through *Tiferet*/beauty, completing the second triangle. If the first triangle (or double triangle) emphasises the head, the second touches the heart. *Tiferet*/beauty stands in the middle of the tree, two channels above it, two below on the central trunk. The association of heart and beauty is profound. We are deeply touched by the beauty in life, its association with time, loss, poignant longing, the ache of being. The beauty of music animates *Tiferet's* soul. I think, too, of Keats: "A thing of beauty is a joy forever". I feel that beauty is one root of ethics, a sense of wanting to do right by life, to do justice to that which can so arouse such depth of feeling (Eigen, 2006, Chapter 1; 2012). On another level, it might not take much for thwarted desire associated with beauty to become destructive.

Capacities work in many ways. If the top *Sephirot* are associated with the head, the second set is associated with the trunk, chest, heart and arms. The *sephirot* take shape along a model of the human body in its upright aspect.

Sephirot means spheres, partly referring to spheres of creation, dimensions, states, capacities. They are aspects of creative processes. They also, mystically, refer to the wheels of Ezekiel's angels, one of the early points of meditation of Kabbalah mystics (the wheels go round and round in all directions, signifiers of spiritual aspiration and possibility). In Kabbalah, flow begins above and goes down, from higher to lower levels, but is not so limited. There is a saying, "As above, so below; as below, so above". The flow goes both ways, all ways. Milner (1957) writes of flow from consciousness downward and simultaneously from below, all reaches of the body, upward. Kabbalah speaks of worlds within worlds, world after world. Wherever one looks, there are worlds of experience and, beyond them, unknown worlds. The way we now picture the heavens, the universe and all its galaxies, systems, and beyond, has similarities to the way Kabbalists pictured aspects of spiritual life.

I feel the verticality of the Kabbalistic tree is a limitation. The vertical provides an important model of experience with deep roots, but is also confining. It is associated with our upright posture, head top, feet bottom, above–below, higher–lower. This links with the vertical dimension of perception: sky or heaven above, earth below, upper and lower strata of society, higher and lower mental and social functions. But there are other possibilities. Deleuze and Guaterri (1987) contrast a rhizome with the vertical tree model. They feel the tree model leads one to think of cause, or origins and effects, or endings, roots below, trunk upright, branch after branch. A rhizome can go every which way, tangles of possibilities, no apparent centre or plan. They emphasise finding oneself in the middle, between, not confined to a linear scheme, no obvious beginning or end.

In *The Psychotic Core* (1986, Chapter 6), I discuss limitations to the vertical emphasis and propose other possibilities of flow. I think now of Leonardo's interest in tangles of hair and trickles of water. Psychoanalysis relied heavily on digestive and reproductive models, both with references to top–bottom (e.g., oral, anal, phallic, genital). These functions and images are not simply confined to top–bottom, but also refer to in–out.

Asian spirituality emphasised respiration, chest, solar plexus, *hara*. The in–out flow of breathing is part of experience that permeates the body. *Kundalini/chakras* are partly organised via top–bottom and bottom-up images, emphasising the rise of the *Kundalini* serpent (psychospiritual energy) from below up the spine, while seated in the lotus position. Body experience exceeds schemas of it. Unpredictable, intangible flows of body sensation, proprioception, kinaesthesia, inklings, intuitive promptings offer possibilities that maps miss. Freud hinted at this when he referred to semi-chaotic, early sensation spreads, which, in his scheme, became more unified with ego development. Still, delicious, if also feared and dumbfounding, sensory possibilities play in the margins of awareness.

Different models reflect different aspects of experience, or ways experience can be organised. A fruitful model pays homage to experience, mines the latter, and opens possibilities. Since experience is so complex and multifarious, different kinds of models, even if they appear to conflict with one another, add to what we can access.

While vertical, the chains of triangles of the Kabbalah tree of life are not necessarily rigid. All *sephirot* communicate with each other, instant interweavings throughout the tree and beyond. There is a children's song: Hashem is here, hashem is there, Hashem is truly everywhere; up–down, all around, that's where He can be found. Hashem literally means the Name (the holy, unutterable, perhaps unknowable and unimaginable name of God). From this vertex, directionality evaporates.

The next triangle, the lowest obvious one (I say obvious, because other triangles, and triangles within and outside triangles, can be postulated that are less immediately obvious) is Netzach–Hod–Yesod. Here, I used the names Splendour, Majesty, Foundation. I have seen schemes where Splendour is with Hod and Majesty with Netzach. Or perhaps they are called something else: for example, Netzach as endurance and determination. There can be a certain amount of shift, interweaving, and reversal. Why, I often wondered, were the lower *sephirot* called majesty and splendour? What does this tell us? If the middle set (*Chesed, Gevurah, Tiferet*) is the chest/trunk, the lower set involves pelvis and genitals and, in part, legs. In a loose sense, this triangle is the Freudian *sephirot*. It makes sense to see reverberations between the edifice Freud constructs from erotic experience and the Kabbalah calling the genital function foundation.

On the one hand, we are speaking loosely, but there is deep fit and resonance.

In its positive aspect, erotic experience is splendour, majesty. There are people who see God during sexual intercourse, some feel like God or a god. It is no accident that so much sexuality is associated with so many gods, East and West. Eros is, or can be, ecstatic. This on a pure level of sensation, or sensation–feeling. Such majesty, such splendour beyond words.

Sensation has received a bad rap in western thought for many years. For Aristotle, God is active reason, active intellect. Sensory life was looked on as lower, disorganised, needing higher functions for formation. Recently, there is more writing on the spontaneous self-organisation of sensory life, without recourse to functions like reason or judgement. And what of the beauty of sensation, all that it gives in colour and tone and inspiration, seeing the wondrous sky, mountains, music that brings uplifting tears, the touch of skin that brings us to heaven. So much sensation is ineffable. Poetry completes it (*Lust*, 2006, pp. 30, 34). The Song of Songs touches, expresses the erotic–divine. There is even such a thing as a God-sensation, a God-feeling. Vast domains and subtle nuances where sensation–feeling blend. Freud saying that consciousness is a sense organ for the perception of psychical qualities is a meditative fount.

Another set of functions and experiences, associated with the "lowest" triangle, emphasises instrumentality, goal-orientated action, drive, plans, seeking and getting and building. This is one reason Netzach is often associated with endurance or determination. We make plans, want something, desire to achieve, make things, accomplish goals (or, as we often say now, live our passions, our dreams). This takes patience, skill, know-how, purpose, learning what leads to what, luck, cause–effect, knowledge of how things work in reality, social–physical space–time. We need Netzach's endurance, stubbornness, persistence and its complement: Hod is often associated with flexibility, more than one way to skin a cat. We take detours, compensate for loss, meet blocks, walls, make substitutions. If Netzach is associated with persistence, Hod connects with plasticity.

Persistence–plasticity: a twinship that has helped us to endure and create.

Nezach–Hod–Yesod: persistence–plasticity and fecundity in action are capacities that not only aid survival, but also can take one towards

God, unite with God, realise godliness on earth. All the *sephirot* are capable of mediating contact with God. All contribute God's presence on all levels of existence. You might say, on a godly plane, all capacities are pure and give rise to divine realisation. But there is, also, smaller use of capacities, selfish, meaner, or narrow-minded use. The Great Spirit, the Great Dream, the Great Plan is, to various degrees, occluded, forgotten, unseen, unheard, unfelt, lost. One is left with a smaller ego at the centre of one's universe, what I want and how to get it, often unsure of what that is. What is I? What is want? Yet, one plunges in, uses whatever resources one has to accomplish what one thinks, feels, imagines are one's goals. Nevertheless, on the plane of human ambition and desire, much good can be done, much achieved of value and worth. Not just know-how, means–end relations, technology, skill, but many kinds of creative activity. It feels good to create, to be creative, to make, to build. *Yesod*/foundation, a driving force at this level, procreation, fertility, genital life signifies generativity in many ways. *Yesod* and all that flows from it partakes in a Generative Spirit. In the human mirror, all capacities are double edged, multi-edged.

Bion (1994b, p. 206) has a way of linking mathematics and geometry with emotions, often emphasising sexual aspects. In one passage, he connects the structure of a triangle with genitals. Not just three (triangular genital areas, or mother, father, baby), but also space, likened to holes or empty space in Henry Moore's sculptures, at once a conjunction of Eros and spirit in emptiness, an encompassing and encompassed emptiness. He speaks of Euclid's "three-kneed thing" and his Pons Asinorum: "the 'elements' of geometry are left behind when the student crosses the Pons". In seamless leaps, he links Euclid, Moore, and Melanie Klein's positions (creative oscillation of breaking apart and coming together): mathematics, art and psychoanalysis enmeshed with erotic, emotional, and spiritual life.

William Blake captures the positive side of *Yesod* in his vision of Lucifer, the morning star, as illuminated. Satan is associated with Energy. Here are some sayings from Blake's "The marriage of heaven and hell".

> Man has no Body distinct from his Soul for that call'd Body is a portion of Soul discerned by the five Senses, the chief inlets of Soul in this age.

Energy is Eternal Delight.

If the doors of perception were cleansed every thing would appear to man as it is, infinite.

Freud's libido is sometimes described as erotic energy that flows, likened to electricity and water, taking many forms. One senses psycho-spiritual overlap with Blake's spiritual vision of the body and Freud's erotic view of spirit. For both, imagination, even hallucination, plays an important role in configuring desire. The flow of divine energy through the *sephirot* is often depicted as a lightning flash in which human energy partakes.

Some corrections and amplifications

My presentation of *Ein Sof* and the *sephirot* means to loosely convey a sense of possibilities, interactions, flows. I have not tried to stick to a rigid scheme (there is no one scheme to stick to; Kabbalah is filled with variations). But I do wish to make some additions and qualifications. While I have tended to emphasise sensation for Netzach–Hod–Yesod, one might better speak of sensation–feeling blends. I hoped to bring out a little of what worlds of sensation offer in their own right. Yet, in a way, sensation is a kind of feeling, a felt sensation. And feeling is a kind of sensation, a feeling sensation. The two are virtually inextricable. *Sephirot* Nos 4–9 (*Chesed* through *Yesod*) are often viewed as the emotional *sephirot*. *Sephirot* Nos 1–3, plus *Daat*, are the "intellectual" *sephirot*. The last, No. 10, *Malkhut*, the realm of action. I find a loose blend of sensation–feeling–action useful in working with *Netzach* through *Yesod*, a kind of instrumental attitude or mode of being, rather than interest in the thing itself. However, even this division does not do experience in these dimensions justice. For example, wondrous sexual moments are values for their own sake, the thing itself. And this can be true of many sensory moments and times of creative immersion, for example, the rapture of scientific discovery.

Loosely speaking, one might view the Kabbalah tree in terms of Jung's four functions: the highest *sephirot*, direct, immediate knowledge, intuition followed (still in the upper *sephirot*) by thinking; the middle *sephirot*, feeling; the lower triangle, sensation. Intuition, thinking, feeling, sensation. The tree adds one more, the lowest, action, which might be symbolised by standing on our own two feet (as happens during Jewish prayer).

One could also make correlations between the lower *sephirot* and Husserl's empirical ego, the middle *sephirot* with Husserl's psychological ego, and the upper *sephirot* with Husserl's transcendental ego.

It is said that only the first three *sephirot* plus *Daat* are intact, the rest are broken. They shattered during the act of creation, unable to take the flow of Divine Energy. The first three plus *Daat* are direct emanations (intuitive conception) from and pathways to God, still whole. In my vision, breakage is progressive, the sensation group (Netzach–Hod–*Yesod*) more broken than the emotion group (*Chesed, Gevurhah, Tiferet*), with *Malkhut*, No. 10, most broken of all.

Nevertheless, it is on the plane of *Malkhut* that our daily human lives take place—life on planet earth, called Kingdom. The Kingdom of real life by real human beings made up of all the enumerated capacities and more. The most broken of all—our kingdom. In the Catholic prayer: thy kingdom come, thy will be done, on earth, as it is in heaven. Here broken, there whole. *Malkhut*, the most broken sphere of all—our home, said to be the end, the point, the purpose of God's creation: the human drama in all its facets. All the higher and highest made for the lowest. What can we do with it? What dare we do with it?

Like the Holy Spirit in Catholic mystical experience, we are given the torn and tattered Shekinah, a feminine aspect of God, with us to help in the work of healing and creative action. She dwells with us in *Malkhut*, giving of her inspirited Presence. In our sphere, torn and tattered, yet beautiful, Queen of Sabbath, with us in travails in the deepest Sabbath point of the soul.

"Holy, holy, holy. The whole earth is filled with Your glory." A vision with which Blake could well concur, which his life and work express.

Broken lives, broken souls. There is a saying, "The whole world is made just for you", our mission, to tend, to mend, to lift ourselves, to give of ourselves. Rabbi Nachman: "Nothing is more whole than a broken heart."

The kind of lifting called for defies the Tree, has no location, dissolves limitations by using them.

Two tales of brokenness: Cain and the Tower of Babel

When Cain killed Abel, he repented. Fear? Guilt? Sorrow? We learn a lot from this murder, speculative learning, important question marks. With Cain, we are already out of the Garden of Eden. We think of the Garden as heaven or heavenly. But was it? Already there was prohibition, threat, temptation. Agitation in the garden. Disturbance. The fall built into the garden, death on the horizon. Murder.

With the promise of heaven comes a fall, a constant conjunction. They go together. With a fall comes murder; first soul murder, then actual murder.

It is a miracle, perhaps underrated, that Cain survived the murder of his brother. To be an actual murderer has at least one virtue or learning. One knows one is a killer. One learns that one can murder. Many deny this possibility. Many think they are not murderers. This might make them more dangerous than Cain. To think one is free of being a murderer is a serious deception.

I think of all the mini-murders one commits daily to oneself and others. And how can one escape murder if one has a baby or is a baby? Mutual murder is part of growing up.

But Cain overstepped a line. Perhaps he had to experience and show what is possible, to live and show a truth.

And what happened? Cain became a builder of cities. On the grave of his brother, cities arose. Cain the builder.

We are leaving out entirely stories of Abel. Able Abel, as they say. Here we note only the conjunction of murder and building, destruction and more life. It is a Kabbalistic tale of life in the world of action, the kingdom of earth, *Malkhut*, where death, destruction, brokenness, and creativity are thoroughly mixed. Just in case you thought you could get away with something and found the kingdom of heaven on earth—the Holocaust, brother killing brother, jealousy, envy, injustice, power injuries throughout the globe today, including the ancient biblical areas. As then, now. As now, then. If I had to summarise in one word what war is about: power. If more words, vanity and existence. And what role did the good God play in this? He set it up, playing favourites, inciting rivalry. A jealous God, possessive, destructive, God of love and justice. As mixed up as earth.

The Tower of Babel story has a similar mix. Here, the destructive nature of God is more obvious, although it is not very hidden in the garden and post-garden dramas. As Bion (1994b, p. 241) relates the tale, the people of earth get together to build a tower to reach heaven. Not a horrendous effort—who does not want to reach heaven? Their attempt to co-operate is destroyed, the tower shattered. Once more the theme of shattering, broken *sephirot*, broken vessels, broken people. Shatter and scatter. The people now are scattered, dispersed, their attempts at unity broken, with the consequence (punishment) of no longer understanding each other's language. One language has become many, understanding broken. Perhaps this latter state is a reference to something deep in the human condition, our lack of ability to understand each other or even to understand ourselves. It highlights difficulties of connection, including connecting with oneself.

The drama moves from unity to dispersal, a basic conjunction. Unity ↔ dispersal. The destructive force is depicted as coming from without (God), as often happens in natural catastrophes or in obvious human violations of one another. But I think it safe to posit a destructive force coming from within the group, within humanity, within ourselves, you and me. We are still far from owning this fact of our nature and far from knowing what to do with it. There is something in us that takes us out of Eden, something in us that destroys heavenly aspirations. This is part of the challenge of *Malkhut*. We like to emphasise a hopeful, creative element, but doing so, true as it is, often diminishes perception of what we are up against. Perhaps it is not heaven we have to worry about, but how to get along on earth. Perhaps the story is warning us against over-idealising a good state, in so far as that prevents us from working with complexities of our reality.

Some meditative notes

Meditative possibilities with the *sephirot* are limitless. Many systems have been worked out. For example, *sephirot* each have numbers, colours, sounds, names of God associated with them. The possibilities are limited only by scholarship and imagination and perhaps a certain spiritual "feel".

Kierkegaard's hierarchical depiction of the man of action, aesthetics, and ethics has some relevance. But what we call "goodness", or "the Good", runs seamlessly through the whole tree as an expression of God's nature. In pure Buddha mind, all capacities depicted are pure. Perhaps especially *Keter*, *Chochma*, *Binah*, *Daat*, and *Chesed*. Here, it is easy to imagine purity of will, wisdom, intuition, and reflection. But we say in God all of these capacities are pure, from earthly generative acts (*Malkhut*) to intuitive union (*Keter*). At the same time, these are human capacities, narratives, representations of godly work through our own disposition and ability. They are projections, also depicted as mirrors of godly tendencies. Whether God or demon is often a matter of context and use. It appears to be human to think of gods and demons. Psychoanalysis is one area engaged in the struggle to expand what we think of as human. To be simply human is complex indeed.

One can meditate on any of the *sephirot*. We can go endlessly deep into any capacity. Pick your *sephira* or let it pick you, quietly attend and you become partner to worlds within worlds, worlds without end. You will envision how any capacity can be evil and/or good in ways that cannot be untangled. You may wish to be good, but if you think you succeed in transcending evil, you are in danger of being a demon.

The whole tree lights up, quivers, trembles. It lights up as whole and in all of its parts. Crystals, rays, indescribable radiance. A great work of the Kabbalah is called *Zohar*, variously translated as radiance, splendour. Any *sephira* takes you beyond itself to the others. You will probably have your own special selections, emphases, organisations, narratives—your own disposition and bent. You might not have the same tree as anyone else.

And *Ein Sof*? The Unreachable? The One Beyond Reach? Closer to you than you are. Perhaps closer to you than you ever will be, unless you find the secret of your identities in the Untouchable Who Touches You. I would like say the Untouchable One, but fear the inevitable, trapped by the gift of language: whether One or zero, zerOne, counting what cannot be counted. The treasure of language with its hints of treasures beyond words and wordlessness.

Bion's (1994b, p. 372) psychoanalytic hint: "The fundamental reality is 'infinity', the unknown, the situation for which there is no language—not even one borrowed by the artist or the religious—which gets anywhere near to describing it".

When I write Bion's "O", his sign for unknowable ultimate reality, I sometimes imagine an opening in the perimeter of the circle (an open system), and then watch it self-erase and vanish.

As with all other avenues, the tree will take you places, and if it takes you well enough along, it disappears.

APPENDIX 2

Four worlds

Four worlds are associated with the various levels of the *sephirot*. The first is *Atzilut* (emanation), the upper tip of the *sephirot*. *Keter* lives here. I might call it a first level of emanation from *Ein Sof*, but, Kabbalah being as intricate as it is, there are finer, less perceptible levels even higher, which we are omitting. *Atzilut* is related to a word meaning close, near. Near *Ein Sof*. A kind of near direct contact, direct enough. The Bible says the soul is pure and Jewish mysticism says a pure point of soul is in contact with God.

There is dispute as to whether *Atzilut*, emanation, is characteristic mainly of *Keter* (crown) or extends to the rest of the "head", *Chochmah, Binah, Daat* (wisdom, understanding, knowledge). Does the second world, *Beriah* (creation), begin with *Chochma* (wisdom), or with *Chesed* (mercy)? For our purpose, I will treat *Atzilut*, emanation, as including the head *sephirot* plus *Daat*, which, strictly speaking, has no location (direct Godly knowledge).

We will posit the second world, *Beriah*, creation, starting with *Chesed* (mercy) and going through *Tiferet* (beauty). Beriah is also related to a word meaning outside, suggesting it is a further step from the primordial infinite Light, which, in *Beriah*, takes the form and function of creativity. Although biblical creation begins with light

("Let there be light"), it is creative light, created light, more formed, differentiated than uncreated Light closer to *Ein Sof*. There is light that we see and dimensions of spiritual Light that we do not see, which are invisible, intangible, non-measurable.

The creative God (the God of creation) is depicted as speaking, "Let there be . . ." and creation springs forth. We have come some way from the wholly unrepresentable and wordless. *Beriah* (creation) is the emotional grouping, chest (treasure chest), arms, solar plexus, creative heart, discernment, judgement, strength.

We will take the third world, *Yetzirah*, formation, to start with *Netzach* (splendour) and go through *Yesod* (foundation). I called this the Freudian grouping, Eros, desire, individual and group will, ego, planning, determination, endurance, flexibility, persistence–plasticity, means–end, causal, achievement. Here, things take new kinds of forms, not just Godly emanation, but human formation. Nevertheless, each of the limiting conditions in the world of formation stems from spiritual attributes. In this scheme, it is difficult to get to a totally godless place, although such a possibility is postulated for the lowest reaches of *Malkhut*. Formative capacities can be exploited by these lowest reaches, but, in our real lives, they are mixed up with everything else.

The fourth world, *Assiah*, action, involves *Malkhut*. *Malkhut*, like all *sephirot*, has many levels, regions, dimensons, and possibilities. It is thought possible—some say experience confirms this—that there exists so low a level that even God cannot penetrate it, a godless place, a godless moment. It is said that in Egypt, the Hebrews reached the forty-ninth level of depravity, had they gone down one more, they would have been unredeemable. This last might seem unimaginable, but many people feel it. There are states of depression and also of evil in which help seems impossible, all is hell. Was it Ortega who said about hell, "Mother church says hell exists, so it must be so. But I don't think Father God ever sends anyone there." I was taught by Jewish mystics that after death the soul goes to something comparable to the cleaners, getting fit for heaven.

Still, one cannot completely escape a sensation that there *is* such a thing as total evil, a realm beyond God and redemption. Yet another sensation says, "I don't believe it".

Freud writes of some energy vanishing in the work of the death drive. He postulates a constant quantity of energy in the psychic universe, yet some of it disappears in psychic death work, perhaps an entropy tendency. William Blake writes, "All states are eternal". Perhaps we can encompass this, for the moment, by using double arrows to express alternating or reversible states: God ↔ no god. God ↔ godless.

I do not mean to paint (pain) a gloomy picture of *Malkhut*. But I feel if we fail to learn more about what to do with our destructive aspects, we will fail to learn what to do with life. *Malkhut*, the world of our activities on planet earth, offers abundance in so many ways, yet death is part of it, and death's mimic, destructive action. In the Middle Ages, the devil was called a clown. In Freud's letters to Jung, Freud called the ego a clown. We had better watch out for what we think, say, and do. When psychoanalysts said a goal was to turn id into ego, a danger sign should have lit up. I would not want my total life, the sum of existence, to be in the hands of my smaller ego and its grasping, destructive proclivities. When Freud wrote the words translated as "beyond the pleasure principle" (1920g), perhaps he ought also to have added, "beyond the lower, lowest ego". What is it in us that can take into account all our proclivities? Is that possible? How? A transcendent function?

I recently saw the film, *A Dangerous Method*, which I found, in many respects, "funny", psychoanalytic fun. For example, the paradox: Jung kept saying he had to go beyond the Freudian emphasis on sexual motivation, yet he was the one who slept with patients. Can the ego with all its desires and ambitions be the guardian against self-deception? Who is fooling whom?

The four worlds might, also, be viewed in terms of Jung's four functions: intuition, thinking, feeling, and sensation. I think of the ancient schema, earth, fire, water, and air, or the four humours, choleric, melancholic, sanguine, and phlegmatic. Four is an attractive number; Jung called it a symbol of unity. Unities keep cracking. I suspect what human beings keep trying to get at is a way to talk about interplay of states and capacities. To this moment, we have not stopped trying.

APPENDIX 3

Circle and rays

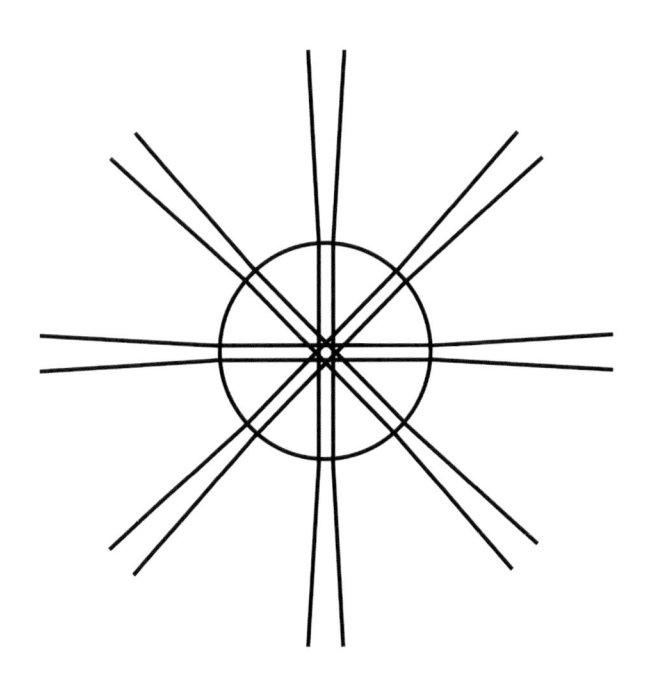

Figure 1. Circle and rays 1.

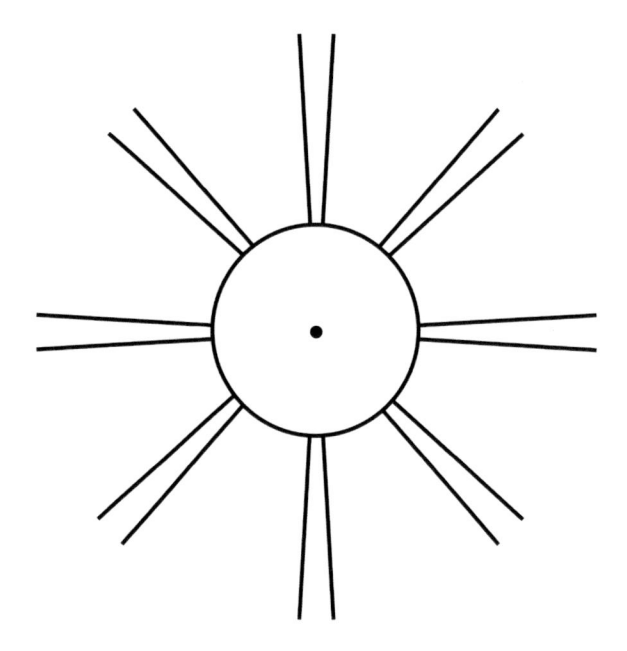

Figure 2. Circle and rays 2.

I drew these diagrams as simple depictions of the idea of many paths through, or somehow associated with, a common centre. One can picture them as radiating out of a common centre or crossing through the latter, emanating from a nucleus, or whatever your imaginations suggest. I was thinking of Nicholas de Cusa's remark about God being a circle with centre everywhere, circumference nowhere. Other translations write God as centre nowhere, circumference everywhere. What is conveyed by either is God everywhere–nowhere. Our perspectives change. Our relationship to Everywhere–Nowhere grows beyond coincidence of opposites.

I do not mean these images as an exact correspondence or representation of Nicholas de Cusa's thought or experience, but as an informal evocation of sensing that parallels aspects of Kabbalah's *Ein Sof*. God is unrepresentable, unfindable, and yet one cannot be anywhere where God is not. Already we are speaking in opposites: is–is not. Bion writes that for a thing to exist it must be and not be at the same time. Nicholas, I think, tries to take us beyond opposites. For Nicholas, language is conjecture. "Knowledge" of God conjecture.

Bion also brings out how our narratives select, slant, and organise experience that exceeds them, subtends them, or has no location at all.

I mean these images in a playful way, to reverie on, to see where they might bring you or what they might make you feel. The geometric nature of them is rigid, as is the *sephirot* tree. They should be wavy or erased, no image at all. But I thought they might be fun and even useful for some. To touch an invisible core without a location anywhere, yet somehow touching us.

APPENDIX 4

O-grams

```
Music      Religion    Sculpture    Poetry     Painting
  |           |            |           |           |
Instrument   God         Stone      Language      Paint
               _____|_____/
                         Root
                          |
                          O
```

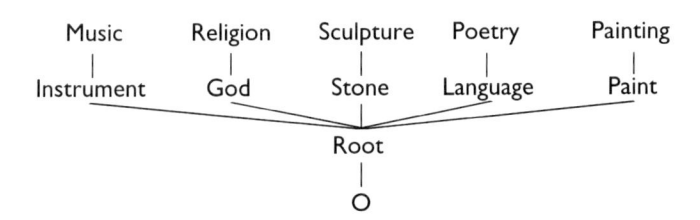

Figure 1. O-gram no. 1 (Bion, 1994b, p. 323).

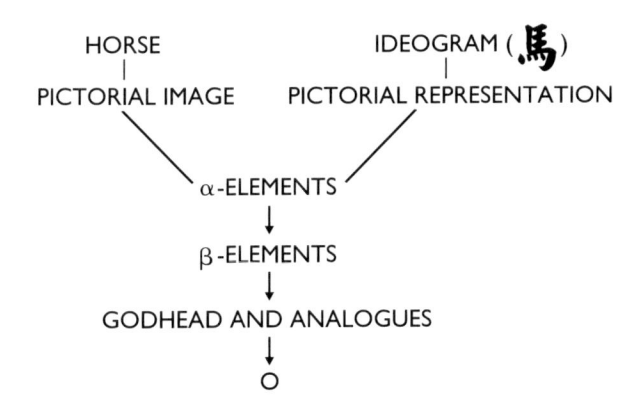

```
    HORSE                    IDEOGRAM (馬)
      |                           |
PICTORIAL IMAGE         PICTORIAL REPRESENTATION
          \                 /
           α-ELEMENTS
               ↓
           β-ELEMENTS
               ↓
       GODHEAD AND ANALOGUES
               ↓
               O
```

Figure 2. O-gram no. 2 (Bion, 1994b, p. 325).

Bion writes favourably about the structure and function of ideograms. He quotes a book that writes of Chinese characters as poetry (1994b, p. 323). He likes the idea of opposites combined in a single image, diverse directionality in a figure. It connotes richness of experience. The ideogram-like hierarchies that he sketched I have called O-grams. Each begins or ends with O alone beneath all processes and branches above it.

In Chapter One (pp. 23–24), I wrote about some of the relationships between Bion's O-grams and the Kabbalah and the structure of the *sephirot*. In O-gram no. 1, O subtends "root", which branches off to instrument, God, stone, language, paint. From a primordial O-sense, tools, spirit, expressive materials (language, paint, stone) emerge, and from these, music, religion, sculpture, poetry, and painting. Bion quotes from Ernest Fenollosa's work on Chinese characters, "My subject is poetry . . ." He gravitates towards expressive gestures, expressive needs, contact with life, and the press to mine what this contact gives rise to. In the beginning, there is O. And O gives rise to experience pressing for survival and culture, a kind of complex monism. By saying, "in the beginning", I have already misappropriated O, which might not have beginning or end.

Note that Bion does not include business or economics or money or the drive for power in this grouping, important as they may be. He includes areas connected with cultivation of emotional life for its own sake, not mainly for instrumental reasons. There may be areas where the two are one, or are connected or stimulate each other, or occlude each other. But in this O-gram there is primacy of emotional expressiveness and the art and religion it engenders.

In Werner Herzog's film, *Cave of Forgotten Dreams*, a documentary about cave drawings in France over 30,000 years ago, one of the scientists interviewed said something like: "Man should not be called Homo Sapiens but Homo Spiritus." The images on the cave were breathtaking, inspiriting and, after all "rational" explanations are exhausted, mysterious. Inspired by spirit, the spirit of inspiration, inspired by O-impacts that compel expressive search and dedication.

We might be killers, but we also are lovers, awe-stricken, touched by wonder and a need to create and express what touches us and the worlds it opens: O-visions.

Meditate on any part of the O-grams and more opens. Follow ripples, and more comes alive, a kind of psycho-spiritual acupuncture massaging dormant soul spots to life. Moments of intensity, appreciation, awakening. In the last sentence on page 323, Bion (1994b) writes, "What is important? The root? The flower? The germ? The conflict? The durability?"

Enter any place, tend it, and gardens, forests, worlds grow. Very like the *sephirot* but the structural analogue to *Ein Sof*, O, is at the bottom, not the top. This is very like the experience I had with Bion when I met him. The instant I walked in for my session, I felt he was under me. It is hard to put this into words. I think of the word "understand", to stand under. I felt him not above but under, a mute support in my painful search. It brought near instant relief, a sense that yes, here was something I could value, a bridge that made my life more possible.

Bion by no means minimises the importance of succession or temporal ordering. In an ideogram, bite/dog/man, it makes a difference whether man bites dog or dog bites man. Nevertheless, a dimension of compression (akin to Freud's "opposite meanings of primal words") plays an important role in experience and psychic ambience. The latter overlaps with domains called "primary process", "syncretic experiencing", "implicate order", "symmetrical mode of being".

In O-gram no. 2, Bion suggests processes spanning a number of dimensions. In the middle of the list are alpha elements, loosely separating things in themselves (beta elements through O) and images. Alpha elements turn things in themselves to images. I put this crudely and wrongly. They no more turn one into the other than one puts feelings into words. Did you ever see someone put a feeling into words? Invisible rabbits into a hat? These are ways of speaking, occluding and alluding to transformational processes incessantly at work. They imply something more graspable and solid than exists. Nevertheless, Bion implies some division between what is above and below alpha.

Again, rudely put, he calls alpha a meaningless term meant to note unknown processes that transform a sense of things-in-themselves into various forms of meaning. We say transforms, but this does not mean the domain of things-in-themselves ceases, disappears into meaning. Perhaps it is better to think of different dimensions of being–experience interacting, taking on many kinds of relations (e.g., antagonism, fusion, reversibility, oscillation, and less tangible auras to which we cannot begin to do justice here).

Note, again, O subtends Godhead and analogues. In a way, this guards "God" from belief systems about "Him". It opens fields of possibilities having to do with what we call mystery. Much of what we say about God is premature closure. This is also true of what we say about no-God. The binary tends to close off what it tries to express.

That beta, Godhead, and O are below alpha, or prior to alpha processing, suggests much goes on that is beyond our range of experience, but profoundly relevant for experience. Much of what has impacts on us might be nameless. To some extent, perhaps we can say impact gives rise to alpha, gives rise to image, gives rise to symbol, gives rise to thought (following and modifying Paul Ricouer).

We now think we know something about electromagnetic fields. For most of the human race's existence, electromagnetic fields were unknown and whatever ways they might have an impact on our life or personalities were unknown. The ancients postulated forces that could have something in common with invisible electromagnetic fields. They gave expression to sensed impact from unknown processes, which they tried to elaborate in imaginative vision and reflection. Impacts of the Unknown and Unknowable played an important role in peoples lives and belief systems. Bion included reference "from infra-sensual to ultra-sensual" in O-gram no. 2. He postulated a "psychoanalytic domain" he likened to Teihard de Chardin's "noosphere" (1959), part of a larger psychosphere, an intangible domain partly sensed by intuition (*Keter*, *Chochma*) but not accessible by common sense or ordinary modes of perception (the lower *sephirot*). Vast unconscious processes modelled not simply on "repression" but on capacities, what we can and cannot access and work with and how. Processes we need to respect even if we cannot know what they are. At the same time, we process what impacts we can and make use of them as we can, through alpha to image, to symbol, to narrative, and thought and vice versa (note that in O-gram no. 2, the arrows point downward from upper functions towards O).

To help keep some brakes on reductionism, Bion adds that taste, touch, smell, sound, and infra-ultra sensuous possibilities can be substituted for image in this schema (just as he notes the different worlds of experience we find through respiration, proprioception, kinaesthesia, digestion, reproduction, and intimations hard to locate of subtle sensory spreads). He hints at vast domains that touch and press us beyond our capacity to access. It is not an accident of our nature that we keep trying to give expression to the unknown on many levels, many ways, with all the capacities we have.

When Bion was in New York, someone asked why he does not use ordinary psychoanalytic language, why introduce a term such as alpha? Bion spoke about how little we know about these processes, then commented, "I use alpha like a nest, hoping birds of meaning might alight". In a way, he turned the *sephirot* upside down, but opened doors of possibility. In the Bible, God is sometimes associated with unknown, inaccessible depths. Bion guards these depths, increases our appreciative sense of them. Dogen (1985), a thirteenth-century Zen master, writes that depth is a measure of height. Measure, here, links with measureless (neither height nor depth). Since both measure and measureless are real moments of being, both important for the way we live, we might place the former in the numerator, the latter in the denominator, the two in one expressive token. Or we might call what is measurable a figure against a measureless background, capable of reversing at any moment.

APPENDIX 5

Bion's Grid

	Definitory Hypotheses 1	ψ 2	Notation 3	Attention 4	Inquiry 5	Action 6	... n
A β-elements	A1	A2				A6	
B α-elements	B1	B2	B3	B4	B5	B6	... Bn
C Dream Thoughts Dreams, Myths	C1	C2	C3	C4	C5	C6	... Cn
D Pre-conception	D1	D2	D3	D4	D5	D6	... Dn
E Conception	E1	E2	E3	E4	E5	E6	... En
F Concept	F1	F2	F3	F4	F5	F6	... Fn
G Scientific Deductive system		G2					
H Algebraic Calculus							

Figure 1. Bion's Grid.

When Bion was in New York (1978), he placed little emphasis on the grid. His main emphasis was on the living session. In experiential terms, he felt the lived session was in row C, dream thoughts, dreams, and myths. If you were D through F, the chances were you were not in the session, not in the felt moment. At most, the grid was for between session reflection about the emotional experience of the lived session, a way of taking a session apart and re-situating it along a number of dimensions that might improve discernment of processes. He wrote of it as a kind of psychic exercise, keeping alpha function alive and in repair, keeping intuition alive.

As he spoke, I wondered if he was consigning the grid to a kind of scrap heap, much the same as Husserl did with his early attempts to mathematise consciousness. Husserl decided that a mathematics of consciousness was not possible (at least from his horizon) and turned full attention to delineating structures of experience and came to be known as the "father of twentieth century phenomenology".

In the New York seminar, Bion also played down his group book (Bion, 1948). When asked about this early, well-known work, he asked, "Are people still reading that?" I am not sure what his tone was. It was not simple—possibly a tinge of disparagement, but more likely amazement or curiosity. I really do not know. I was taken aback by it myself. Later, I wondered if there was some latent disappointment. After all, it was 1978, some thirty years later, and so many papers on psychotic processes of individuals had been published, the great works of the 1960s climaxing in *Attention and Interpretation* (1970), not to mention his last long work in the 1970s, *A Memoir of the Future* (1991), and the seminar that was going on at that very moment. Yet, I doubt it was disappointment or chagrin. It really sounded like surprise, at once pleasurable and curious.

I know many people for whom the group book *is* Bion. That is the book they know and read and value, the vast and stunning literature that followed notwithstanding. It is as if the latter, with few exceptions, never was. But there are others for whom the unfolding chain of work is revelatory, ongoing in his last year.

I personally like the group book (*Experiences in Groups*, 1948, republished by Tavistock, 1961). It begins like a Pinter play, a single spotlight on the analyst alone on the stage. Gradually, patients enter and interactions begin. The analyst, who felt all right alone, now begins to undergo various pulls and tugs, emotional deformations under the pressures of group engagement. He tries to pinpoint some of these deformations, describe them. A mini-dictionary of basic assumptions and the forces they exert begins.

I would not want to lose the early work. And I would not want to lose the grid. To say Bion has gone further is not to take away from each step achieved.

I take up the grid here because I loosely connect it with the *sephirot*. It is not a one-to-one connection. There are important differences. But there is overlapping ambience and concern. What I say is not definitive, just reflective conjectures, more tentative exploration than conclusive. Saying this clears the way for me to take some poetic licence and risks.

Others have written about the grid in more detail than I do here, but I want at least to give a broad sketch for the interested reader who might find the lines of letters, numbers, and words bewildering, even attacking.

The vertical axis, A to H, is often characterised as growth from more concrete to abstract thought. The binary concrete–abstract occludes too much and I will try to portray some intricacies. The horizontal axis, 1 through 6...n, portrays growth of experience towards action, leaving the way open for unknown possibilities beyond action. The terms delineated seem crude compared with processes they express. The grid as a whole can be taken to portray growth of thought, experience, and feeling. I propose that it explores growth of sensation as well. The forest can easily be lost in the trees, so before I get bogged down in details, let me say the whole grid quivers, trembles, is aglow. It shakes like jelly, ripples, and, like the *sephirot*, any part can link with any other and all parts are contained in each other. All parts of the grid, like the *sephirot*, express transformations.

Note that O is missing. Everything on the grid proposes to express O-impacts and, in one or another way, gives them shape or prepares them for shaping. As soon as there is impact, it is subject to transformational processing through whatever filter systems our life form is made of and uses. O is slanted through the "grid" of our makeup. One way of saying this is that we have access to what our system does with O-impacts. The O of the O-impact, so to speak, is unknown.

The grid begins with beta-elements, "A" on the vertical axis. Above A is a blank. For me, this suggests that a lot of processes go on off the grid, before reaching the grid, before reaching beta. Let us be a little wild, and posit *Ein Sof* off the grid. Instead of reaching the grid through *Keter–Chochma*, the head, it reaches it through beta, more akin to what the ancient Greeks called *hyle*, a kind of substance or matter subject to transformation. Beta is often spoken of as "sensation", a problem being how sensation grows towards thought. One might say, the grid roughly parallels the *sephirot* upside down, with *Keter–Chochma* at the bottom. But things are not so simple.

In psychosis, thoughts can act as sensations and be taken as real things, the things themselves. Thoughts, images, and hallucinations become reality. Bion spends a lot of time in his work delineating these processes. Thoughts, feelings, and sensations transform into animated presences, inspirited reality.

The grid opens the larger question of how things function. All locations on the grid represent functions. How does a thought or feeling or sensation function? Does it function as a beta object or alpha element, a dream or myth or preconception, conception, concept? Every thought one meets does not function as a thought, is not necessarily part of an ongoing thinking process. Concepts can function as demons or airy nothings or enter a struggling, genuine attempt to think. As hinted above, boxes on the grid can fuse or dissociate in myriad ways.

In one of their positive functions, beta objects feed alpha function. Raw registering of impact attracts and stimulates psychic work. The work might be to shut out the impact. Or continue registering it, unconsciously getting inklings about it, implicit hypotheses (A1), reaching towards notation, attention, enquiry, and action on the horizontal plane and towards dream/mythic images–narratives, preconceptions, conception (F1) on the vertical. In this mode, some speak of an alpha-betising function, converting beta impacts through alpha function into material more usable for growth of experiencing.

I wrote of *hyle* in relation to beta, and one can usefully meditate on the "materiality" of beta impacts, parallel with what Aristotle might have meant by *hyle*. But I would add here a kind of psychic "materiality", unknown psychic material, part of unknown psychic processes, which undergoes transformations through image, symbol, and thought, as the O-grams try to signal.

A good part of the literature on beta-objects emphasises their negative aspects, how they interfere with emotional processing. "Agglutinated" or demonised beta objects block and destroy psychic flow. They exacerbate persecutory reactions and are projected or evacuated, attempts to get rid of them, creating further persecution.

Bion depicts O-impact as a catastrophic big bang, destroying psychic space, creating a situation in which psychic objects hurtle through expanding space in a more and more unhinged manner. To some extent, vertical column 2, the Psi function, slows things down, a kind of braking system or contact barrier, permeable but resistant. This enables notation and attention and enquiry on the one hand, and dreaming, mything, and various implicit–explicit thinking processes on the other. He is graphing creativity.

The birth of psychic life is depicted in a trauma mode, but capacities for creative work with trauma develop. Bion frequently writes of a "choice": to deny or modify. The grid suggests creative work has no end. It might also have no beginning. The grid is a depiction of possible creative processes against an unknown background. I suggested above that much goes on off grid before appearing on grid. I spoke of the missing O as *Ein Sof* off the grid, infinitely unknown, but you can substitute whatever you think might be a better designation of unknown O.

Bion attributes unknown processing to alpha, which plays a role near the beginning of emotional digestion. One function needed is notation. Bion gives the example of recording a happening with images. Images function like ideograms containing vast complexities of a moment, often expressed as opposites as binary narrative develops. The latter makes use of, and develops, operations such as compare–contrast, same–similar–different. But he is adamant in calling attention to unknown work going on in growth of emotional processing from the beginning.

Like Kafka, who calls his life an incomplete moment, Bion feels that most dreams are aborted dreams. Dreams (row C) play a role in emotional digestion. For example, they try to work with catastrophic impacts, but often short-circuit before a "solution" is found. Most people experience dreams that suddenly break off before a conclusion. Perhaps the breaking off is itself a "conclusion", portraying a sense of our fragmented and incomplete existence. In *Damaged Bonds* (2001), I wonder if part of human irritability is associated with widespread emotional indigestion. What kind of dream will a therapy session be? Can therapy play a role in emotional digestion, or end as another nightmare?

Bion feels nightmares serve an important function, potentially drawing awareness to emotional trauma. He sees it as an advance to be able to produce a nightmare rather than a somatic symptom to express what frightens one.

Yet, with everything we know about dream and defensive operations, Bion keeps the field open. What is attempting to be processed how? For Bion, we are explorers. If the emotional background of our being is unknown infinity with a million faces (experienced/filtered through dread, agony, rage, joy), we are ever partners with endless unfolding/development.

I write of beta objects as mediating raw impacts of O, an impact that can take on many emotional colourings as processing develops. We do not know what beta objects are. They are something Bion made up to avoid knowing something we do not.

Sometimes, I represent them as raw trauma globs, as yet unspecifiable, undefined, awaiting processing and/or evacuation. Alpha somehow works on them, turning them into material useful for learning, growth. An immaterial material, since they are psychic events which cannot be located like a liver or brain (one can see brain processes represented by video images, but no one has ever "seen" a thought. One thinks thoughts, senses feelings).

I tend to see beta as very alive, dense with compacted possibility. I think of the Tao master referring to himself as uncarved stone. Or Michelangelo's "prisoners", semi-emerging yet still part of the rough stone that is their uncarved background and substance. Or the simple child at the Passover *seder*, who does not know enough to ask, a kind of mute mystic silenced by the overwhelming nature of things, dumb with awe. Or myself as a child, who often felt, "What's going on here?" A kind of dumb, quiet state, blank, waiting. I did not have a clue what was happening until college, when suddenly the light in the rock began to shine. I have felt like a beta object all my life or, at least, in touch with a beta dimension of existence (pre-existence?).

Another trope for beginnings of emotional processing might be life emerging in a swamp or marsh, or deep in the sea, mysterious odd forms that fascinate and repel.

Fascination with origins is not new in history. Ancients had notions of the unformed, the potential. Bion underlines processes that make up the things themselves, not simply order imposed from without: self-organising and self-destroying processes, interacting with other processes.

In Appendix 1, I wrote about the positive contributions sensation makes in the aliveness, flow, and colour of life. Sensation is not a dull clod, an inert beta object. It can be ineffable, lifting existence. It plays a role in feeling feelings, sensing thoughts. Freud called consciousness a sense organ for perception of psychical qualities. This is an important component of Bion's work, the feeling of life. How does life feel? A sense of life. What is your sense of your life? A question about the micro-infra-world Bion tunes into involves not whether x is beta or alpha, but how does it function? For example, is it moving towards life, or life-destructive at a given moment? Freud would say, always both. How does one envision this?

Sometimes, the grid is pictured as functioning in reverse. Instead of a mute sense or intimation growing towards action–thought, the latter devolves back into nothing, or worse than nothing (Eigen, 1996, Chapter Five, "Bion's No-thing").There are malevolent and positive nothings, a negative and positive grid, depending on how a state or capacity is functioning, often both positive *and* negative working together as well as seemingly at cross purpose. Freud said that every psychic act is made up of both life and death instincts—the negative–positive grid is one translation of this vision. This is very like creative–destructive functions of the *sephirot*, bringing the soul towards God *and* towards alienation (remember how agonised Rabbi Nachman was when feeling so close *and* so far from God; above, Chapter Two). Or another, less deist plane, a double movement towards worthwhile existence *and* self-destruction (Eigen, 2001, Chapter Six, "The need to kill oneself").

The grid lends itself to many uses. For example, it can stimulate musings on relations between action and thought. Action is the last filled-in horizontal category, and features of thought the last on the vertical. They are conjoined in processes signified by A through F. Action can dominate thought or thought dominate action, with many mixtures and variations. Husserl describes thought as a mental act. Action applies to many realms. A range that includes and extends beyond beta element acts might be called alpha function acts, dream acts, on through varied degrees and qualities of higher thought-influenced acts. The same can be said on the scale of thought-driven action, for better or worse, depending on the kind of thought and action. We are ridden with evil imaginings and ideas. Thoughtful does not necessarily mean good, or acting bad. The reverse is often so.

At the "highest" thought level on the grid, there is practically no interaction with the vertical column or, for that matter, with anything other than itself. An exception is G2, which has a braking function. For the rest, "higher" thought can go where it will, unconstrained by anything but itself, although Bion has taken care to call attention to emotional aspects of thought in general. At the top and bottom we reach empty space, openness. Yet, one cannot say H is unconditioned. The whole mass of processes, from A through F, subtend and lead up to it. Bion feels there are emotional substrata of mathematics (we saw a little of this earlier, discussing triangles in Euclid; above, Appendix 1). Even the leap into no-constraints has invisible links with unknown processes "before" and "after", or no location in time at all. The grid, then, is like Michelangelo's prisoners, carved out from a larger unknown horizon, which Bion likens to Teilhard de Chardin's noosphere, a topic discussed in Appendix 6 (Stefanie Teitelbaum, in conversation, originally alerted me to the profound significance of Michelangelo's "prisoners").

APPENDIX 6

Bion quotes

Following is a selection of quotes from Bion that are relevant for psycho-spiritual reflection. One could say most of Bion's work is, so why pick these? I have picked a few that contain some kind of more or less explicit reference to psychological and spiritual dimensions. There are many more. I hope, from the few I chose, to stimulate interest for further exploration. I hope, too, that when I add some notes that they will be more helpful than annoying.

* * *

> The fundamental reality is 'infinity', the unknown, the situation for which there is no language—not even one borrowed by the artist or the religious—which gets anywhere near to describing it. (1994b, p. 372)

* * *

Bion uses O to signify unknown infinity, ultimate reality. In this book, I have linked it with *Ein Sof* and YHVH, realities no name, image, or conception can circumscribe or describe. Yet, to use O, *Ein Sof* or

YHVH seems harshly limiting. In the passage above, Bion tries to leave it open, no sign for it at all, although words like "the fundamental reality, infinity, the unknown" already infringe as pointers. What is it Buddha tries to convey when he speaks of reality that words or images or concepts cannot do justice to, not even words like "emptiness"? The unknown, too, is part of science and problem solving, gaps in knowledge and attempts to fill them. The physicist, Eddington, somewhere said about the universe, "Something unknown is doing we don't know what".

The difficulty one has representing what cannot be represented applies to ordinary communication as well. There is inbuilt frustration in trying to communicate feelings, even communicating them to oneself. Frustration often tinged with pleasure, perhaps, but difficulty. One struggles to find words to say what one means or even to take a stab at knowing what one means. As one looks more closely, difficulties representing the Unrepresentable mark the work of emotional communication more generally. Frustration that is part of the attempt to commune–communicate often is taken for granted, or inadequately recognised, making it harder to appreciate this aspect of our situation. It is not uncommon to think we have successfully communicated something important to us, only to be taken aback by layers of misinterpretation. Misrepresentation–misinterpretation is part of our attempt at linking. What we thought we said or hoped to say often fades as speaking and listening happens, running like water through our fingers. We admire the poet who can create reality as he speaks, opening and stabbing our hearts.

* * *

> Psycho-analysis itself is just a stripe on the coat of the tiger. Ultimately it may meet the Tiger—The Thing Itself—O. (1991, Book 1, p. 112)
>
> I shall suppose a mental multi-dimensional space of unthought and unthinkable extent and characteristics. Within this I shall suppose there to be a domain of thoughts that have no thinker. Separated from each other in time, space and style, in a manner that I can formulate only by using analogies taken from astronomy, is a domain of thoughts that have a thinker. This domain is characterized by constellations of alpha-elements. These constellations compose universes of discourse that are characterized by containing and being contained by

terms such as, 'void', 'formless infinite', 'god', 'infinity'. This sphere I shall name by borrowing the term, 'noosphere' from Teilhard de Chardin [*The Phenomenon of Man*], but as I wish to avoid too great a penumbra of associations, particularly those activated by the term, 'sphere', I shall employ a sign that is as devoid as I can make it (compatible with retention of its capacity for communicability), sigma. (1994b, p. 313)

* * *

First, "a mental multi-dimensional space of unthought and unthinkable extent and characteristics". Within this larger space, "a domain of thoughts that have no thinker".

The above constitutes beta-space. Meditate on "a mental multi-dimensional space of unthought and unthinkable extent and characteristics" and see where it takes you. Also, "thoughts without a thinker".

One might think of "a mental multi-dimensional space of unthought and unthinkable extent and characteristics" as the larger realm, a background horizon without imaginable time or compass. Within that realm, thoughts without a thinker. In another passage, when discussing the O-grams (1994b, p. 326), Bion calls the unthinkable domain and thoughts without a thinker a psychosphere.

Within the psychosphere is what Teilhard de Chardin called the noosphere. For Teilhard de Chardin it was a further step in evolution, from the physical world, or geosphere, to the animate, or biosphere, to the human mind and makeup which evolves into the noosphere, a unifying, connecting mental–spiritual network (perhaps a parallel to Indra's net in Buddhism). Noosphere comes from Nous, mind–spirit in ancient Greek philosophy. For Bion, it is a part of the psychosphere that begins thinking thoughts, vast thoughts and survival thoughts, incipient alpha space. As mentioned in his quote, he renames Teilhard de Chardin's noosphrere, sigma. It might also be that he used Teilhard de Chardin's Omega (the final "point" of evolution), O, as a general sign for unknown infinite, ultimate reality.

Teilhard de Chardin, a Jesuit palaeontologist, described each successive stage as emergent realities. For Bion, that might be so, but they tend to function more as simultaneously existing structural processes complexly interacting with (or, in the case of one of his astronomical images, racing away from) each other. The more general unthinkable psychosphere, and its domain of unthought thoughts—both subsumed in the category of beta-space—remains as a kind of infinite background and horizon as alpha-space, sigma, and thoughts with a thinker develop. Bion gives as examples of constellations of alpha-elements vast thoughts like "void", "formless infinite", "god", "infinity". Thoughts about the unthinkable. A good deal of human thinking reaches towards the unthinkable.

Alpha function opens a path towards thinking about psychological life without confining it to a visible body. Terms like "mood", "character", "personality", "anxiety" point to realities that are not identical with physical identity. Similarly, for Bion, psychoanalytic realities constitute a "psychoanalytic domain" (1994b, pp. 325–326) which is not accessed by ordinary thinking or discourse, but requires development of a special capacity for intuition, characterised by being without memory, desire, understanding, and expectation.

The latter might be an impossible state, yet is a direction or path, a way of exercising a specific capacity, even stimulating its birth and development. Alpha-space is capable of growth, its limits unknown. You can develop your own links, similarities, and differences with intuition in Jewish mysticism and the *sephirot*. Remember, each *sephira* includes and communicates with all other ones, so that intuition (represented by higher *sephirot*) can function to investigate and work with lower "spheres" as well as to open paths towards "that" beyond all spheres.

For Bion, it is harder to tell what is higher or lower and, if he could, I suspect he would eliminate hierarchical directionality from descriptions of psychic space, realities, and possibilities. Communication with the language we have is very demanding, especially when we try to use it to express something it was not made to express. Bion writes of the difficulty of using a frame of mind and discourse that grew up in the service of survival for illuminating psychological concerns, issues of integrity, and personal development.

Mind keeps trying to blow itself up, go beyond itself, shed shells. I think of diverse images from East and West: Moses seeking to free a people from slavery. The biblical trope involving freedom from slavery in Egypt links to a word, *mitzrayin*, related to limit, limitations—freedom from limitations. For a Christian gloss on the same theme, Nikolai Berdyaev, *Slavery and Freedom* (1975), faith in Christ as a freeing path. For Buddha, freedom from slavery to our minds, life, disposition, and tyranny of self.

What kind of seeing, experiencing, intuiting, vision is discovered and is in the process of discovery?

Development of psychoanalytic intuition poses challenges for practitioners. Intuitive sensing, vision, or processing can make an individual more sensitive to psychotic ranges of experience. So much of what an everyday individual slides past, hides, ignores, versions of self, identities taken for granted, might open access to feared psychotic processes. Intuition contacts "pellucid" and "turbulent" areas of sigma, opening windows the personality tries to seal.

Intuition opens worlds unperceived by the habitual self. For example,

> dreams would need to be thought of as belonging to a far more widely extended C category [see Appendix 5, Bion's Grid], much more extended than one enclosing only visual or any other sensuous images, though in 'practical' psychoanalysis only elements within the sensuous range would, by definition, be experienced. Sooner or later, the investigation would have to be extended to infra- and ultra-sensuous areas first, then from noosphere to psychosphere. (1994b, p. 326)

To try to evoke a sense of what he points to, Bion writes of big Sigma and small sigma, the latter referring to the flesh and blood person we see before us, the former to unseen, unknown psychic realities. (1994b, pp. 313–317). All our capacities come into play, work at once. All the knowledge (K) we gain from ordinary philosophical and scientific cognition, and domains of "inaccessible" realities revealed by faith (F). Bion calls F the psychoanalytic attitude, radically opening to the unknown.

The practical me writes unknown in a process sense, although mystical me might mean more. Bion writes that in a session he is concerned with what he does not know, the unknown. Once he knows, there is more unknown. Opening of vistas that cannot be exhausted can be a source of depression for the patient. Just as the patient thought he solved the puzzle of his personality, infinities of unknown areas are sighted, dots of the Unknowable.

A lot of work goes on without quite knowing (K) what it is. One may sense something, an intimation, a felt change, without knowing what it is. Something is happening, we may say. Something is happening we as yet have no words for. In the Lankavatara sutra, much transformation goes on without language, image, conception. Bion's sign, T in O, links with such processes. F in O and T in O. Faith in unknown ultimate reality and unknown transformations going on in the latter.

> Job: Yea, though You slay me, yet will I trust You.
> Jesus: Eli, Eli, why have you forsaken me?

Perhaps both speaking of a death suffered in the birth of intuition. Perhaps both speaking of the Great Death suffered in the depths of faith.

Buddha, too, expresses a transformational journey, *samsara*—nirvana, suffering–well being (heaven, equanimity, awakening, bliss, peace beyond understanding . . .). We might see Buddha as one possible signifier of a resurrected state, not so much the redemptive moment as the moment achieved, post-redemption. He sought to remove a "thorn from his heart" and is said to have felt he did this (Blomfield, 2011): a thorn with a long history and many names.

* * *

> These poets and artists have their methods of recording their awareness of some sort of influence, stimuli that come from without, the unknown that is so terrifying and stimulates such powerful feelings that they cannot be described in ordinary terms . . . We need to invent some form of articulate speech that could approximate to describing these realities, the phenomena that I cannot possibly describe. (1994b, p. 369)

* * *

The sentences left out of the preceding quotation had to do with situating experiences that Bion was pointing to sub-cortically—"thalamic" experiences "with no real synaptic communication between the thalamus and the subsequent development of the mind". He had been speaking of realities communicated by Tennyson, Shelley, and Keats, but also a direct hit of a tank in the unit he helped command: "bodies were charred and blackened, and poured out of the door of the tank as if they were the entrails of some mysterious beast of a primitive kind which had simply perished then and there in the conflagration" (1994b, p. 368).

He went on to talk about the mystery of a word like "Yaveh", whose meaning, spelling, and pronunciation are unknown-unknown

> because nothing else could possibly do any sort of justice to the fact that 'Yaveh' was a way of talking about a force, a power that cannot be described in articulate speech such as is appropriate when talking about omnipotence or omniscience, or the ordinary formulations of religion—none of them adequate ways of describing the matters to which attention is to be drawn by the communication. (1994b, p. 370)

It is freeing to think that the ordinary ways we speak of God do not come close to the mysterious experience touching us. Such words eclipse the experience they try to communicate, reducing it to fantasy or wish-fulfilment—ah, to be omnipotent, omniscient. Thank God, we are not. Bion tries to clear what we call God of these dilutions and pollutions. (See the section, "God's personality" in *Rage*, Eigen, 2002.)

* * *

> Many mystics have been able to describe a situation in which it is believed there really is a power, a force that cannot be measured or weighted or assessed by the mere human beings with the mere human mind. This seems to me to be a profound assumption which has hitherto been almost completely ignored, and yet people talk about 'omnipotence' as if they knew what it meant and as if it had a simple connotation. Martin Buber [1970] came much closer to recognizing the realities of the situation when human speech is resorted to ... When one talks about 'I–You', the significant thing is not the two objects related, but the *relationship*—that is, an open-ended reality in which there is no termination (in the sense that this is understood by ordinary human beings). The language of ordinary human beings is only appropriate to the rational, can describe only the rational, can only make statements in terms of rationality. (1994b, p. 371)

* * *

> Any particular religion changes with the prevalent fashion, but the fundamental thing, religion itself, does not. It is a very powerful force, as can be seen by the evidence of what would appear to be a sign or symptom of the thought of a period dug up by the archaeologists who excavated the Death Pit of Ur. Apparently, when the ruling authority died, the court also died with him; they were all buried in the same pit and took the same dose of whatever was used before they were buried

alive. That in itself would seem to suggest that the religious force is a very powerful one, whether it is located in God, or the people, or the priesthood, or the court authorities. (1994b, p. 374)

* * *

I add the above quote to emphasise that the unknown Bion alludes to is not "controllable" by language or desire. It seems monstrous; it seems divine. Or it exceeds all categories. In the *Bhagavad Gita*, Krishna makes a monstrous appearance, yet is in all things and more— *is* all things. In part, the "monstrousness" has to do with human perception and awareness being unable to take full dosage of divinity/reality. We see many demons and monsters in Buddhist art, having to do with demonic tendencies in life and mind, but also with deformations of vision owing to lack of capacity to take too much intensity of experience, a theme Bion emphasises. In the Bible, we are told to see God is to die. One way we tend to translate this is that seeing God leads to a kind of death of narrower vision, opening big-vision.

Literature about Job in recent years tends to emphasise his slavishness to God, being cowed by show of strength. In one translation, he never stops arguing, never gives in to God's evil. In one of my own "takes", I feel Job has cut away everything, coming upon the One remaining and, in a burst of spontaneous awe and miraculous apprehension, is thrown past speech into the thing itself, the very Moment God Appears, contact with the Unknown. Cutting away everything is a movement of contraction; his new life, new family, new land represents a movement of expansion after the Amazing Vision and Contact, Moment of Reality of Realities. When we come back down to earth, we are left with our questions, yet also something more.

In another "take" or state, it is hard to get past the reality of evil, mine, yours, ours, humankind's. In psychoanalysis, we take little nibbles at a time, although sometimes we go overboard and find ourselves being eaten, both chewed and swallowed whole, by the great monster in one of its profiles.

* * *

When the patient said he dreamed he was being swept down the river to the weir—"I tell you, I never woke up so fast in my life."—what, according to me, was he talking about? In so far as I know, I was in a state of mind in which I am wide awake. Is that 'wide' enough? Or is it a state of mind that is too narrow—like 'to–fro tender trambeams' truckling 'at the eye'? [Gerard Manley Hopkins, "The Candle Indoors"] Or too 'wide' awake, too conscious, too rational?

'By that window'[*idem*] what sights did the patient see that made him 'wake up' so fast that he could not be swept down the stream? Was it the danger of becoming, like me, too wide awake? Or, like me, too fast asleep—in fact, the sleep of death? Or in the state of mind of 'sleep' of psychoanalysis?

'There plant eyes, all mist from thence purge and disperse, that I might see and tell of things invisible to mortal sight'. [Milton, *Paradise Lost*, Book III] But the price appears to be the loss of 'mortal' sight. It cannot, however, be bought by 'losing' mortal sight; to be blind, unconscious, unaware of the world visible and audible, where you are in the 'yin' state of mind, is not the solution. One must dare to be aware—consciously—of the universe that is apparent in the state of mind in which one is asleep and the state of mind appropriate to 'awake'. Yin and Yang. Therefore merely being able to concourse musically, balletically, athletically, is not enough; it must be an intercourse—a means of communication 'inter', between two states of mind. Socrates described himself as a mental midwife; perhaps the psychoanalyst is a midwife between two states of mind of the analysand. (1994b, pp. 366–367)

*   *   *

A term like 'love' cannot describe something even as well as the term, 'the love of God'—that at least makes an attempt to introduce an element that shows it is not a discussion about something that is so simple as physical love known to the human animal. A lioness nuzzles and shows every sign of feelings of love and affection—if interpreted in human terms—for prey it has destroyed; but it is murderous love, the love that destroys the loved object. Such visual images may be used to talk about love, even what we imagine to be mature love, but there is some other love that is mature from an absolute standard. This other love, vaguely adumbrated, vaguely foreshadowed in human speech, is of an entirely different character; it is not simply a quantitative difference in the kind of love one animal has for another or which the baby has for the breast. It is the further extension to 'absolute love', which cannot be described in the terms of sensuous reality or experience. For that there has to be a language of infra-sensuous and ultra-sensuous, something that lies outside the spectrum of sensuous experience and articulate language. It may be approximated to by methods of communication that are not purely sensuous; the artist who paints a little street in Delft can see and communicate a reality to the observer who then sees something that is quite different from any brick wall or little house that he has ever known or seen in his life. Even in science, Heisenberg's description of the Uncertainty Principle shows that already a crises has arisen—a 'crise de foi'. (1994b, pp. 371–372)

* * *

All my life I have been imprisoned, frustrated, dogged by common-sense, reason, memories, desires and—greatest bug-bear of all—understanding and being understood.

This is my attempt to express my rebellion, to say 'Good-bye' to all that. It is my wish, I now realized doomed to failure, to write a book unspoiled by any tincture of common-sense, reason, etc. (see above). So although I would write, 'Abandon Hope all ye who expect to find any facts—scientific, aesthetic, religious—in this book', I cannot claim to have succeeded. All these will, I fear, be seen to have left their traces, vestiges, ghosts hidden within these words, even sanity, like 'cheerfulness', will creep in. However successful my attempt, there would always be the risk that the book 'became' acceptable, respectable, honoured, and unread. "Why write then?" you may ask. To prevent someone who knows from filling the empty space—but I fear I am being 'reasonable', that great Ape. Wishing you all a Happy Lunacy and a Relativistic Fission . . . (1991, "Epilogue")

APPENDIX 7

Rabbi Nachman's paths

The following summarises what I am calling "paths" that Rabbi Nachman lived at various moments of his life. They condense aspects of his spiritual experience written about in Chapter Two, above, and in Green's (2004) *Tormented Master: The Life and Spiritual Quest of Rabbi Nahman of Bratslav*, which I draw from. Do not be confused by the different spellings of Rabbi Nachman's name. Green uses Nahman; others like Kamenetz (2010), also a background source for Chapter Two, use Nachman. I use Nachman because I grew up spelling the gutteral throat growl-like sound "ch". Neither spelling conveys the actual sound in Yiddish or Hebrew.

While elaborations are in Chapter Two, I thought a list of Rabbi Nachman's paths might be helpful. The list is not meant to be complete but suggestive.

* * *

1. *Emotions as messengers*. Nachman enjoyed and suffered intensities of experience, moments of closeness to God and moments of ghastly separation, unbridgeable distance. His states echo emotions in the psalms, the psalmist bereft, cast into the abyss when

God withdraws, joyous when again God's face shines. A kind of double movement of towards–away. One does not know when God withdraws or the soul withdraws, and vice versa. Whichever extreme he lived, Nachman felt emotions as paths to and from God.

2. *Incubation.* Nachman felt there was a time to be silent, to hide, withdraw from company or, at least, minimise full exposure of what was brewing. Often it was important to nourish secret inner processes, to let them germinate. Premature exposure could damage them, aborting potential spiritual life.

3. *Constant struggle.* This can be inner and/or outer struggle. Struggle with one's own personality and struggle with the world. There comes a time to come out and struggle with the world, a time when such struggle not only urges one to give expression to oneself, but stimulates further growth. Nachman frequently remarked that he was always growing, going further, not making do with status quo. He felt a spiritual developmental imperative.

4. *Nature and music.* Like the Baal Shem Tov, Nachman valued communion with nature, which was soul nourishing in many ways. He felt all nature alive with song. Shepherds who sang nourished the grass, which nourished the lambs. Singing, clapping hands to the rhythm of prayer, dancing, all expressive of Divine Presence, soul nourishment. Spirit comes alive through song. This reminds me of King David dancing and the music of the last psalms. It is said that Nachman danced with such intensity that you could not see him move, his stillness was so profound. His dancing created and discovered new dimensions in stillness.

5. *Suffering.* Wittgenstein said there were certain sufferings that led to experiencing God. He would have found a companion in Nachman on this score. The deep pain of life, existential suffering, the acute agonies of trauma, loss, and grief, but also spiritual sufferings, longing for the Divine. Nachman traced an ache that ran through many levels, an ache that raced after God, the latter receding the closer the aching heart came. This ever-present gap ensured always going further. Just as one thought one was as intimate as one could get, intimations of still greater intimacies invited the soul.

While *suffering* seems to be part of path no. 1, emotions as messengers, I felt impelled to give it space of its own, given the emphasis Nachman placed on a certain aching longing in transitional movement towards God. Bion, too, writes of the importance of suffering experience. He tends to mean suffering the build up of experience, gradually tolerating more of its intensity, and even speaks of suffering joy. Dewey, in *Art as Experience* (1936) writes of difficulties in tolerating the build up of intensity while viewing a work of art. To suffer rather than deny or disown experience is a problem cutting across many dimensions of life.

6. *Confession and prayer.* These two each deserve a category of their own but I find it natural to bring them together. Prayer takes many forms, an abyss of silence, stillness of peace and awe, expressions of thanks, and supplications of all sorts. So many ways of seeking God, communion with God. Song and dance can be part of prayer, so can weeping, shouting, and begging.

    Nachman places special emphasis on confession. Not just during prayer, but confessing aloud to one's spiritual teacher. Confessing everything that is in one, all doubts, agonies, apprehensions, needs, disappointment, longing, hurt, anger, and fear. It sounds like a relative to free association in psychoanalysis.

    Prayer, too, can be a form of confession, and confession a form of prayer. Nachman goes further, urging his followers to speak from their hearts, from their broken hearts. Further yet, to break their hearts in prayer and confession. He advocates praying in your native tongue, the language that comes naturally to you, not necessarily Hebrew. God understands you, whatever language you speak, so speak the language that best conveys what is in your heart, the language of the heart. A Nachman saying: "Nothing is more whole than a broken heart".

7. *I Don't Know.* At times Nachmen felt his knowing, not just his learning, but inspired teaching of the moment, a knowing that suddenly burst forth with light, could make people faint with spiritual apprehension, beauty, awe. Such bursts of holy light might be too much for those not ready. One reason Nachman ordered unpublished writings of his to be burned had to do with his fear of the harm they might cause to a world not ready for such heights of illumination. He feared they would do more ill than good.

At other times, he felt he knew nothing. Sometimes abjectly, distraught, out of contact, not tuned into the Divine current. Yet other times, he said, "My knowing is great, but my I don't know is greater". He confessed to the most profound not-knowing, or non-knowing, as a path. While he supported the unlearned in whatever they knew, he urged the learned to confess non-knowing. None of us know in face of God and the workings of Life—none of us know. Our faith has intimations and takes us to unknown places. The unknowing linked with faith does psycho-spiritual work our knowing could not have imagined: Bion's F in O and T in O.

APPENDIX 8

Selected readings

This section of selected readings supplements the References. I thought it might be useful to readers to include works that help form a background for what is presented. Some are cited in the text, many not. The list is partial and suggestive. Kabbalah literature is vast. What is included and left out is largely chance and circumstance. One book not mentioned is the Bible. Its stories, laws, psalms, prophecies, images, and possibilities form a core basis for Kabbalistic meditation. The suggestion that Moses saw God and spoke with Him face to face is a mirror image of a reality we find within ourselves.

Basic background readings

Buber, M. (1987). *Tales of the Hasidim: The Early Masters Vol 1*. New York: Shocken Books.
Eigen, M. (1998). *The Psychoanalytic Mystic*. London: Free Associations (especially Chapter Three, "Infinite surfaces, explosiveness and faith").
Scholem, G. (1996). *On the Kabbalah and Its Symbolism*. New York: Shocken Books.

Other suggested readings

Bakan, D. (2004). *Sigmund Freud and the Jewish Mystical Tradition*. Dover Publications.

Besserman, P. (1997). *Kabbalah and Jewish Mysticism*. Boston, MA: Shambhala.

Bion, W. R. (1970). *Attention and Interpretation*. London: Karnac, 1984.

Bloom, H. (1984). *Kabbalah and Criticism*. New York: Continuum.

Carlebach, S. (1996). *Shlomo's Stories: Selected Tales*, S. Yael Mesinal (Ed.). Lanham, MD: Jason Aronson.

Dick, P. K. (1991). *The Divine Invasion*. New York: Vintage.

Eigen, M. (2002). *Rage*. Middletown, CT: Wesleyan University Press.

Eigen, M. (2010). *Eigen in Seoul* (Vol 1): *Madness and Murder*. London: Karnac (for "brokenness" see Day 3, Afternoon).

Epstein, P. (1978). *Kabbalah: The Way of the Jewish Mystic*. New York: Barnes and Noble, 1988.

Friedman, M. (1988). *A Dialogue with Hasidic Tales: Hallowing the Everyday*. New York: Human Sciences Press.

Green, A. (2004). *Tormented Master: The Life and Spiritual Quest of Rabbi Nahman of Bratslav*. Woodstock, VT: Jewish Lights.

Heschel, A. J. (1984). *The Sabbath*. New York: Farrar, Straus and Giroux.

Idel, M. (1990). *Kabbalah: New Perspectives*. New Haven, CT: Yale University Press (only if you read Scholem).

Kamenetz, R. (2010). *Burnt Books: Rabbi Nachman of Bratslav and Franz Kafka*. New York: Schocken Books.

Keilson, H. (2010). *The Death of the Adversary*, I Jarosy (Trans.). New York: Farrar, Straus and Giroux.

Langer, J. (1976). *Nine Gates to the Chassidic Mysteries*. New York: Berman House.

Matt, D. C. (1995). *The Essential Kabbalah: The Heart of Jewish Mysticism*. San Francisco, CA: Harper.

Matt, D. C. (Trans.) (2004). *The Zohar* (Pritzker Edition). Stanford, CA: Stanford University Press.

Schachter-Salomi, Z., & Miles-Yepez, N. (2009). *A Heart Afire*. Philadelphia, PA: The Jewish Publication Society.

Schneerson, M. (1996).*Torah Studies*. Brooklyn, NY: Kehot Publication Society.

Steinsaltz, A. (1994). *The Thirteen Petalled Rose*. Lanham, MD: Jason Aronson.

Zalman, S. (1973). *Likutei Amarim: Tanya*. "Tanya". Brooklyn, New York: Kehot Publication Society. (Caution: this book may burn you with hidden flames.)

Recent works by psychologists/psychotherapists on Kabbalah and psychology

Berke, J., & Schneider, S. (2008). *Centers of Power: The Convergence of Psychoanalysis and Kabbalah*. Lanham, MD: Jason Aronson.

Drob, S. (2009). *Kabbalah and Postmodernism*. New York: Peter Lang (Sanford Drob's website on Kabbalah and psychology: www.newkabbalah.com/sanford.html).

Starr, K. (2008). *Repair of the Soul: Metaphors of Transformation in Jewish Mysticism and Psychoanalysis*. New York: Routledge.

REFERENCES

Balint, M. (1959). *Thrills and Regressions*. London: Hogarth Press.
Berdyaev, N. (1975). *Slavery and Freedom*. New York: Scribner.
Bion, W. R. (1948). *Experiences in Groups*. London: Tavistock, 1961.
Bion, W. R. (1970). *Attention and Interpretation*. London: Karnac, 1984.
Bion, W. R. (1991). *A Memoir of the Future*. London: Karnac.
Bion, W. R. (1994a). *Clinical Seminars and Other Works*, F. Bion (Ed.). London: Karnac.
Bion, W. R. (1994b). *Cogitations*, F. Bion (Ed.). London: Karnac.
Blomfield, V. (2011). *Gautama Buddha: The Life and Teachings of the Awakened One*. London: Quercus.
Buber, M. (1970). *I and Thou*. New York: Charles Scribner's Sons.
Chuang Tzu (1964). *Chuang Tzu: Basic Writings*, B. Watson (Trans.). New York: Columbia University Press.
Deleuze, G., & Guaterri, F. (1987). *A Thousand Plateaus: Capitalism and Schizophrenia*. Minneapolis and St. Paul: University of Minnesota Press.
Dewey, J. (1936). *Art As Experience*. New York: Perigee, 2005.
Dogen (1985). *Moon in a Dewdrop: Writings of Zen Master Dogen*, K. Tanahashi (Ed.). New York: North Point Press.
Eigen, M. (1986). *The Psychotic Core*. London: Karnac, 2004.
Eigen, M. (1992). *Coming Through the Whirlwind*. Wilmette, IL: Chiron.

REFERENCES

Eigen, M. (1993). *The Electrified Tightrope*, A. Phillips (Ed.). London: Karnac, 2004.
Eigen, M. (1995). *Reshaping the Self: Reflections on Renewal in Psychotherapy*. Madison, CT: Psychosocial Press.
Eigen, M. (1996). *Psychic Deadness*. London: Karnac, 2004.
Eigen, M. (1998). *The Psychoanalytic Mystic*. London: Free Association Books.
Eigen, M. (2001). *Damaged Bonds*. London: Karnac.
Eigen, M. (2002). *Rage*. Middletown, CT: Wesleyan University Press.
Eigen, M. (2004). *The Sensitive Self*. Middletown, CT: Wesleyan University Press.
Eigen, M. (2005). *Emotional Storm*. Middletown, CT: Wesleyan University Press.
Eigen, M. (2006). *Feeling Matters*. London: Karnac.
Eigen, M. (2007). *Conversations with Michael Eigen*. London: Karnac.
Eigen, M. (2009). *Flames From the Unconscious: Trauma, Madness and Faith*. London: Karnac.
Eigen, M. (2011). *Contact With the Depths*. London: Karnac.
Eigen, M. (2012). Beauty and destruction: can goodness survive life and what would that mean? Paper presented to the First World Humanities Forum, Busan, Korea, 25 November 2011.
Eigen, M., & Govrin, A. (2007). *Conversations With Michael Eigen*. London: Karnac.
Fliess, R. (1973). *Symbol, Dream and Psychosis*. Madison, CT: International Universities Press.
Freud, S. (1920g). *Beyond the Pleasure Principle*. S.E., 18: 7–64. London: Hogarth.
Freud, S. (1937c). Analysis terminable and interminable. S.E., 23: 211–253. London: Hogarth.
Green, A. (1992). *Tormented Master: The Life and Spiritual Quest of Rabbi Nahman of Bratslav*. Woodstock, VT: Jewish Lights Publishing.
Grotstein, J. S. (2007). *A Beam of Intense Darkness. Wilfred Bion's Legacy to Psychoanalysis*. London: Karnac.
Kamenetz, R. (2010). *Burnt Books: Rabbi Nachman of Bratslav and Franz Kafka*. New York: Schocken Books.
Klein, M. (1997). *Envy and Gratitude*. Vancouver: Vintage Books.
Levinas, E. (1999). *Alterity and Transcendence*, M. B. Smith (Trans.). New York: Columbia University Press.
Meltzer, D., Hoxter, S., Bremner, J., &Weddell, D. (2008). *Explorations in Autism*. Strathtay, Perthshire: Harris Meltzer Trust.

Milner, M. (1957). *On Not Being Able to Paint*. Madison, CT: International Universities Press.
Milner, M. (1987). *The Suppressed Madness of Sane Men: Forty-four Years of Exploring Psychoanalysis*. London: Routledge.
Schachter-Salomi, Z., & Miles-Yepez, N. (2009). *A Heart Afire*. Philadelphia, PA: The Jewish Publication Society.
Schneerson, M. (1998). *On the Essence of Chassidus*, Y. Greenberg & S. S. Handelman (Trans.). Brooklyn, NY: Kehot Publications Society.
Scott, W. C. M. (1975). Remembering sleep and dreams. *International Review of Psycho-Analysis*, 2: 253–354.
Teilhard de Chardin, P. (1959). *The Phenomenon of Man*. London: Collins.
Winnicott, D. W. (1992). *Psychoanalytic Explorations*, C. Winnicott, R. Shepherd, & M. Davis (Eds.). Cambridge, MA: Harvard University Press.

INDEX

Abel, 89
Abraham, 56, 59
Adam, 10, 48, 56
affect, 23, 65
  aborted, 23
  intensity of, 26
affective
  attitudes, 11, 77
  life, 9
  state, 23
  world, 23
aggression, 34, 49–51, 55–56
Akiva, Rabbi, 12–13, 39–41
Allen, W., 29
anger, 15, 27, 34, 67, 127
anxiety, 21, 28, 48, 118
  separation, 27–28
Aristotle, 10, 62, 85, 110

Baal Shem Tov, 10, 41, 46–47, 57–58, 126
Balint, M., 17, 133
ben Eliezer, I., 10
Berdyaev, N., 118, 133

Bible, The, 4, 15, 39, 52, 56, 63, 82, 93, 105, 122, 129
Bion, W. R. (*passim*)
  alpha
    elements, 25, 103, 116, 118
    function, 25, 108, 110, 113, 118
    space, 117–118
  beta
    elements, 25, 103, 109, 113
    impacts, 110
    objects, 110, 112–113
    space, 117–118
  cited works, 7, 19, 21–23, 25–26, 30, 41, 75, 86, 90–91, 101, 103, 108, 115, 118–119, 121
Faith, 20–23, 26, 42–43, 45–46, 63, 65, 120
Grid, 23–26, 107–111, 113–114, 119
  A, 109, 113–114
  C, 108, 111, 119
  D, 108
  F, 21, 42–43, 45, 76–77, 108, 113–114, 119–120, 128

H, 109, 114
K, 20–21, 23, 76–77, 119
O, 19, 21–23, 25, 42–43, 45, 62, 66, 77, 78, 92, 102–104, 109, 111–112, 115–117, 120, 128
T, 43, 77, 120, 128
O-grams, 22, 26, 66, 101–102, 110, 117
Blake, W., 19, 44, 69, 86–88, 95
Blomfield, V., 120, 133
Boehme, J., 5–6, 60
Boris, H., 49
Bremner, J., 27–28, 134
Buber, M., 76, 121, 133
Buddha/Buddhism, xi, 4, 16, 24, 35, 37, 43–44, 56, 68, 79, 91, 116–117, 119–120, 122

Cain, 89
Campbell, J., x
catastrophe, 7, 20–21, 25–26, 31–32, 41
  emotional, 42
  imminent, 22
  natural, 90
  psychic, 41, 61
Catholicism, 49
Chassidic/Chassidus, 2, 4, 7
Christ(ian), xi, 2, 80, 118
Chuang Tzu, 43, 66–68, 133
conscious(ness), 28, 53, 64, 73, 76, 83, 85, 108, 113, 123
  awareness, ix
  control, 43
  dreaming, 16
  mathematics of, 108
  painful, 28
  semi-, 53

Dalai Lama, 4
death, 13, 16, 35, 43, 71, 80, 89, 94–95, 120, 122
  drive, 15, 48, 94
  instinct, 48, 113
  psychic, 95
  sleep of, 123

de Cusa, N., 98
de Leon, M., 40–41
Deleuze, G., 83, 133
depression, 32–33, 47, 53, 94, 119
  position, 32
Deri, S., 8–9
development(al), 23, 112, 118, 120
  challenge, 8
  ego, 84
  of psychoanalytic intuition, 119
  personal, 118
  spiritual, 126
Dewey, J., 76, 127, 133
Dogen, 105, 133

Eddington, A., 18, 22, 116
ego, 42, 86, 94–95 *see also*: development(al)
  -centric, 42, 48
  empirical, 88
  psychological, 88
  super, 72
  transcendental, 88
Eigen, M., x–xi, 3, 7, 11, 18–19, 21, 27–28, 30, 63, 67–68, 75, 78, 82, 113, 121, 133–134
Ein Sof, xi, 7, 18, 22–23, 26, 31, 61, 79–82, 87, 91, 93–94, 98, 103, 110–111, 115
Einstein, A., 49
Eros, 21, 85–86, 94
Eve, 48, 56

fantasy, 6, 27, 29, 30–32, 35, 41, 51, 79, 121
Fliess, R., 28, 134
free association, 24, 59, 127
Freud, A., 72
Freud, S., x–xi, 9, 15–16, 24, 32, 34–35, 44, 48, 50, 54, 59, 63, 65, 67, 69, 72, 76–77, 84–85, 87, 94–95, 103, 113, 134

Garden of Eden, 89
Ginsberg, A., 77

Gnostic(ism), 5, 40
God (*passim*)
  broken/severed, 9
  creative, 5, 94
  -head, 25, 104
  jealous, 89
  of Genesis, 5
  Olympic, 33
  Yosemite, 11
Govrin, A., x, 134
Graham, M., 5
Green, André, 30, 72
Green, Arthur, xi, 47, 64, 125, 134
Grotstein, J. S., 21, 134
Guaterri, F., 83, 133
guilt, 27, 48, 89

hallucination, 87, 110
  psychotic, 76
Hasidism, 10
hate, 11, 65–66, 69–70 *see also*: self
Herzog, W., 25, 102
Hindu, xi
Holy Land, 47
Hoxter, S., 27–28, 134
Hussein, S., 6, 19

Idel, M., 40
I–It, 76
I–Thou, 76

Jesus, 52–53, 60, 63, 65, 82, 120
Job, 15, 21–22, 42, 45, 63, 65, 120, 122
Judaism, xi, 12, 16, 41, 62

Kabbalah, ix–xi, 1–2, 4–5, 9, 11–12, 15, 20, 22, 25–26, 32, 35–36, 39–40, 54, 59, 62, 74, 83–84, 87, 91, 93, 102 *see also*: *Ein Sof*, Tree of Life
  Lurianic, 5, 19, 41, 59
  mystics, 83
Kamenetz, R., xi, 46, 51, 125, 134
Kastel, Rabbi, 3, 74
Kellner, Rabbi, 2–3, 73–74

Kiefer, A., 7
King David, 56, 58, 126
Klein, M., 6, 20, 32, 35, 44, 48, 77, 86, 134
Kohut, xi, 35
Krishna, 122
Kuan Yin, 44–45
Kundalini chakras, x, 84

Lacan, J., xi, 72
Levinas, E., 77–78, 134
Levy, D., 24
life (*passim*) *see also*: affective, Tree of Life
  anxieties, 28
  divine, 81–82
  emotional, x, 23, 25, 42, 75, 77, 86, 102
  human, 17
  instinct, 113
  process, 9
  psychic, 7, 19, 31, 49, 61, 111
  spark of, 11
  spiritual, x, 57, 83, 86, 126
  waking, 16
Los Angeles Psychoanalytic Society, 72
Luria, Rabbi, 5–8, 41, 59–60, 62
  see also: Kabbalah

meditation, 5, 13–15, 24, 26, 36–37, 40, 50, 55, 58, 62, 68, 83, 85, 90–91, 102, 110, 117, 129
Meltzer, D., 27–28, 134
memory, 71
  traumatic, 28
  without, 21, 42, 76, 188
Messiah, 58–60, 74
metta, 12, 36
Miles-Yepez, N., 58, 135
Milner, M., ix, xi, 22, 64, 83, 135
Moses, 51, 66, 118
mother, 16, 27, 29–30, 35, 46, 52, 86
  baby–, 29
  new, 35

Nachman, Rabbi, xi, 20, 41–43, 45–49,
    51–59, 62–66, 68, 71–73, 77–78,
    81, 88, 113, 125–127
New York University Postdoctoral
    Contemplative Studies Project,
    ix
noosphere, 104, 114, 117, 119

object, 27
    beta, 110, 112–113
    loved, 123
    of interest, 66
    psychic, 111
    relations, 121
    use of, 29
Oedipus, 32
    pre-Oedipal, 32
O-grams *see*: Bion, W. R.
omnipotence, 6, 19, 121
    phony, 19
omniscience, 6, 18–19, 121
Other, 16, 25

psyche, x, 8, 11, 47, 54, 62, 75–76, 78
psychic, 24, 33–34, 36, 85, 94
    act, 113
    ambience, 103
    capacity, 8
    catastrophe, 41
    death work, 95
    energy, 44
    events, 112
    exercise, 108
    flexibility, 36
    flow, 110
    force, 44
    functioning, 73
    heartbeat, 24
    life, 7, 19, 31, 49, 61, 111
    material(ity), 110
    objects, 111
    organisation, 75
    origins, 19
    path, 67
    process, 110
    qualities, 113

reality, 48, 54, 62, 68, 118–119
resources, 9
seeing, 76
shattering, 19
space, 11, 31, 111, 118
symptoms, 25
taste buds, 58
threat, 28
womb, 54
work, 34, 110
wormhole, 78

rage, 11, 49, 73, 112
    helpless, 49
    impotent, 49, 73
Rangell, L., 72

Saint Augustine, 21
Saperstein, S., xi
Schachter-Salomi, Z., 58, 135
Schneerson, M., 7, 11, 58, 135
Scott, W. C. M., 50, 135
self, xi, 11, 24, 32, 36, 46, 56, 60, 74,
    119
    centred, 34
    -deception, 95
    denigrating, 55
    -destroying, 113
    -erase, 27, 92
    expansive, 6
    -feeling, 7
    habitual, 119
    -hate, 32
    -identities, xi
    -organisation, 85
    -organising, 113
    -states, xi
Sephirot, 22, 31, 37, 64, 79, 82–84,
    86–87, 90–91, 93–94, 102–103,
    105, 109–110, 113, 118 *see also*:
    Tree of Life
    broken, 88, 90
    creation, 65
    emotional, 87
    Freudian, 84
    intellectual, 87

lower, 84, 88, 104
middle, 87–88
tenth, 7
upper, 83, 87–88, 118
Sewell, E., 49
sexual, 33, 73, 85, 87
aspects, 86
desire, 73
interpretation, 48
motivation, 95
nature, 55
transcendence, 48
sexuality, 48, 85
lack of, 48
Shakespeare, W., 69
Shekinah, 7, 61, 88
Shimon bar Yochai, 40
Sholem, G., 40
Spotnitz, H., 33
Statman, A., 51
Sufi, xi
symbol(ism), 44, 77, 88, 104, 110
of unity, 95

Talmud, 34
Taoist, xi, 6
Teilhard de Chardin, P., 114, 117, 135

Torah, 2, 4–5, 39–40, 54, 63, 66
Tower of Babel, 17, 24, 89
Tree of Life, 7, 22, 31, 61, 79–80, 84, 87, 99
Tustin, F., 9

unconscious(ness), 28–29, 53, 110, 123
phantasy, 6
process, 104

Vital, C., 5

war, 34, 55–56, 89
atomic, 18
Cold, 18
Second World, 17
Weber, S., 12
Weddell, D., 27–28, 134
Wentworth, D., ix
Winnicott, C., 29, 31
Winnicott, D. W., x–xi, 16, 27–30, 33, 35, 45–46, 62, 66, 72, 135
World Trade Center, 47

Z dimension, 16, 46
Zohar, ix, 34, 40–41, 91